MY JOUR

Lots of love,
Hannah
Green
x

MY JOURNEY HOME

Overcoming Homelessness and Post-Traumatic Stress Disorder

Hannah Green

Cherish
EDITIONS

First published in Great Britain 2021 by Cherish Editions
Cherish Editions is a trading style of Shaw Callaghan Ltd & Shaw Callaghan 23
USA, INC.
The Foundation Centre
Navigation House, 48 Millgate, Newark
Nottinghamshire NG24 4TS UK
www.triggerpublishing.com

British Library Cataloguing in Publication Data
A CIP catalogue record for this book is available upon request
from the British Library
ISBN: 9781913615154
This book is also available in the following eBook formats:
ePUB: 9781913615161

Cover design by More Visual
Typeset by Lapiz Digital Services

Cherish Editions encourages diversity and different viewpoints. However, all
views, thoughts and opinions expressed in this book are the author's own and
are not necessarily representative of us as an organisation.

All material in this book is set out in good faith for general guidance and no
liability can be accepted for loss or expense incurred in following the information
given. In particular this book is not intended to replace expert medical or
psychiatric advice. It is intended for informational purposes only and for your
own personal use and guidance. It is not intended to act as a substitute for
professional medical advice. The author is not a medical practitioner nor a
counsellor, and professional advice should be sought if desired before embarking
on any health-related programme.

In memory of Leah

12 March 1990–5 August 2019

For anyone who has ever faced any form of injustice

This book is a wonderful story of hope and belief. Hannah is an extraordinary lady, a fighter who has come through some times that would have finished me. I have nothing but admiration for Hannah, a young lady who has shown a fantastic spirit when it would have been easier to give up.

If you're going to read one book this year, make it this one – a beautiful tale of hope, belief, determination and pure spirit, which eventually beats a path for Hannah to free herself and help others. My respect and admiration as always.

Neville Southall MBE

ABOUT THE AUTHOR

Hannah Green is the Lived Experience Specialist at the Centre for Homelessness Impact. Her role involves ensuring that real experiences of homelessness are linked to evidence and data, and are at the heart of everything the Centre does.

She also works as a freelance writer and journalist for publications such as Novara Media and HuffPost. She speaks regularly at a range of different events and conferences and spends most of her free time surfing. Hannah is also a volunteer with the Wave Project – a surf therapy charity that uses surfing to help young people improve their emotional and physical wellbeing.

You can follow her on Twitter: @h_green21

CONTENTS

CHAPTER 1

ROCK BOTTOM HAS A CELLAR

17 December 2018.
I was ready to end everything.
I couldn't deal with living anymore.

The flashbacks were too overwhelming, the nightmares kept me up all night, and I knew the bad memories would never go away. I'd been suffering in silence for two months after returning from abroad, and life had come to a complete halt. I had nowhere to live, and most days I couldn't function like a normal person. I was drinking way too much, wasn't socializing, and had completely given up on everything.

It was a Sunday night and freezing cold. I was driving at 70 miles per hour towards Filey, and I'd made up my mind. The thought had been in my head for a few weeks, but now, that was it – time to stop all the pain.

I slowly increased the speed of my car. I was strangely calm about the decision I had come to; soon, it would all be over. The things I'd been through as a child that I'd never been able to tell anyone about would finally be gone; I wouldn't have to face up to them, and I wouldn't have to keep on pretending that I was only struggling with PTSD from a sexual assault while at university.

Just as I was about to turn the steering wheel to send the car crashing into a tree, a police van pulled out in front of me. Looking back, I'm not sure why it stopped me, but I'm glad it did. I went back to my cousin Courtney's house, and, after telling her what had nearly happened, she was instantly on Google trying to work out what to do with me. She made me send an email to a local mental health resource centre and an hour later I was standing outside the Crisis Cafe of Scarborough Survivors. Courtney had threatened to ring the police if I didn't speak to someone. It's safe to say that Scarborough Survivors' Crisis Cafe saved my life – both that day and several others.

But how did I get to this point?

CHAPTER 2

THAT NIGHT

I started university in York in 2015, and from the beginning I struggled with anxiety and missed quite a few lectures. I'd been struggling with anxiety for a few years, ever since I'd started to question my sexuality, along with the "thing" that I'd never spoken about to anyone (and never intended to).

I'd come out as gay in 2014, and things had settled down a bit after that. While at university, I kept in contact with a group of old friends, who I saw regularly: Shannon, who I'd been friends with since primary school, and two male friends from college.

I've never written about "that night" before. The night that changed everything. It is a memory that will be scarred on my brain forever. A memory that I can never forget, but that I am slowly learning to live with. I think that's the hardest part – you come to realize you can never forget, it can never be erased, and it will never just magically go away.

The day before, Mothering Sunday 2016, Shannon, me and "Brad" (not his real name) met up to watch Brad's younger brother play football. Most of that day is a blur now, but I know we went back to my house, had tea, watched a James Bond film with my family, and went to bed at a reasonable time because I had university the next day. Brad had stayed at my house several times before. The following morning, Dad took me and Brad to York, where I went to my lecture and he headed home; we planned to meet up again when I finished that afternoon.

It was a beautiful sunny Monday. My lecture finished a little after 5pm, and Brad and his grandad picked me up from university. I remember the car journey absolutely terrified me: Brad's grandad was elderly, which you could tell from his driving, and he swerved from lane to lane on the dual carriageway on the short journey to his house. We had fish and chips for tea, and then watched *Cool Runnings* with Brad's parents and brother. I can't watch that film anymore. I'd slept at Brad's house before, on a mattress on the floor. He was one of my best mates and I trusted him with my life. His parents went to bed and we went to watch *Kingsman: The Secret Service* in his room (another film I now can't watch). He offered to sleep on the mattress, and I wasn't going to turn down the bed. At some point we decided to turn the film off and get some sleep. I rolled over and tried to sleep, expecting him to move to the mattress on the floor. But he didn't. He went on to sexually assault me.

I froze. I repeatedly said, "No", "Stop" and "I don't want this", but I couldn't move. I tried to scream, but nothing came out. What was happening? Brad knew I was gay. Brad considered himself a Christian.

I jumped up, grabbed my phone and locked myself in the bathroom. I opened Facebook and, knowing it was late, looked down my contact list to see who was online. One name stood out; I'd been friends with her for a few years and knew that she sometimes worked in York until late. I sent her a message, and I think she realized that something wasn't right, even though I didn't say what was wrong. I sent her my location and she promised to get there as fast as she could.

I left the bathroom, grabbed my hoodie and bag, and said that I was going to sleep downstairs. Brad was clearly terrified; he was crying, asking me if I'd rung the police, and threatening to kill himself. He could tell I wanted to leave. I went downstairs and he followed, still crying and repeatedly apologizing. He said he was going to get me a duvet from upstairs, and when he came back down, he disappeared into the kitchen. I heard keys jangling but didn't think much of it. As soon as he went back upstairs, I went to the kitchen to find the house keys – they were nowhere. Brad must have hidden them.

I spent at least 15 minutes searching for a key for any door or window. I got a text from my friend; she was outside, but I still couldn't get out. I texted Brad and told him that if he didn't let me out I would ring the police, and my friend outside threatened to smash a window.

Brad came downstairs, grabbed a kitchen knife and threatened to stab himself; I thought he was going to turn it on me. I told him I didn't care; he could do it but it wasn't going to change anything – it wouldn't change what he'd just done.

He ran upstairs and came back down with his mum, who could see how upset I was but seemed completely oblivious to what had actually happened. He was shouting about how we were best friends and that he loved me. I was falling to pieces and begging them to let me out. Eventually, his mum made him give me the keys after I made it clear my friend would be smashing a window if they didn't. I left, leaving some of my belongings behind.

I ran down the street to the car, where another friend was also waiting. They could tell I wasn't okay. I didn't say much, and they didn't pry. We went back to our friend's student digs in York, where my friend offered me her bedroom. I immediately locked the bedroom door, and have no idea where my friends slept that night.

I woke up early the next morning, as if it had all been a terrible dream. It was only when I realized how much pain I was in that I understood it had really happened. I rang my mum, still in shock, and told her something bad had happened the previous night and my friends had picked me up.

I'd slept in my clothes, I didn't brush my teeth or have a shower, and walked straight to my morning seminar as if nothing had happened. For half an hour or so I was fine – then it hit me. I couldn't breathe. I walked out and headed to the nearest window. I felt trapped. I ended up sitting in the corner on the floor, crying my eyes out, and trying to figure out what to do.

I was obviously in distress, and this caught the attention of a cleaner. He sat next to me on the floor and asked me a few questions. I didn't say much at all but he managed to work out what had happened from my mumbles. He kindly went and got me a cup of tea and rang my brother, who was at college on the other side of York. My brother dropped everything to come and pick me up.

Once I was home, the days just seemed to fade into one, and the next week was a complete blur.

CHAPTER 3

THE AFTERMATH

I didn't tell my mum specifically what happened that night, and we never really had a proper conversation about it, but I'm guessing she worked it out. I went back to university a week later, and again sat in the lecture hall as if nothing had happened. I listened, took notes, but nothing really went in. Around halfway through the lecture was the first time it happened…

> *I am there, in his room. It is happening all over again.*
> *He is on top of me, I can't move. I can't even breathe.*
> *Everything hurts.*

I was having a panic attack. I grabbed my stuff and flew to the door. Once I was outside, I found a seat and managed to calm myself down. I sat for ages, trying to work out what had just happened; nothing made any sense. The lecture finished and everyone left. The lecturer came out and asked me if I was okay. I tried to explain that I wasn't and that something bad had happened, but I wasn't making much sense. I think he knew I was overwhelmed, so he suggested we go somewhere quieter. Once we were in a private room I became extremely upset, but somehow managed to get across what I needed to say. I was so grateful that he didn't ask too many questions. He went to get one of the female lecturers, who also treated me gently and respectfully.

I spent most of that day in a haze. The lecturers arranged for me to see the Head of Student Services later that day, and I waited anxiously for hours in the same room. I was trying to work out what was going on in my head. By the end of the day, I had an appointment organized at the local sexual assault referral centre (SARC) later that week.

At this point I think I was in denial about what had happened. Rape is something you're warned about as a teenager. Something you're led to believe is perpetrated in dark alleyways by men you don't know, when you've had too much to drink and lost your friends. Surely it couldn't happen somewhere you've been before, somewhere you felt safe, by someone you knew, while stone-cold sober? But that could not be further from the truth; your attacker can be someone you trust – a friend, a partner – or, for a mere 7% of rapes, a stranger. Surely this couldn't happen to me. One of my best friends wouldn't do that... would he? Not someone who had stood by me for two years and whom I trusted with my life?

The "thing" I mentioned before started to play on my mind a lot more during the aftermath of the assault, but I tried my hardest to push it to the back of my mind.

I didn't go back to university for a few more days; and when I did return, my mum drove me there and waited for me. I was terrified of being in York; what if I bumped into him? He knew where the university was – what if he came to find me? I became scared of my own shadow, and wouldn't go anywhere on my own. My family were great – they took me everywhere I needed to go, helped me with the most basic things, and just supported me.

CHAPTER 4

DECISIONS

Before visiting the SARC (sexual assault referral centre), I hadn't really thought about reporting what happened to the police. My friend Charlotte drove me to the appointment. It was only after I had told the woman at the SARC what had happened, who said I could choose to report it at a later date, that the seriousness of the assault hit home. I gave her the clothes I had been wearing "that night", in case I decided to report, and told her I would think about it. Looking back, I can see I was still in shock. The whole day was like an out-of-body experience, as if I was watching myself.

Charlotte took me to the beach to try to cheer me up after having to talk about what happened. We only spoke a little bit about what I should do – my head was all over the place and I needed to switch off.

Later that week, the woman I spoke to at the SARC put me in contact with both an independent sexual violence advisor (ISVA), who arranged to come and visit me a few days later, and the sexual health clinic in York, so I could get checked out.

At this point, alongside university, I was working at a local secondary school as a PE technician – teaching kids how to climb, and assisting with other lessons when members of staff were off sick. I missed a few days that week, and when I turned up the following Monday I had to have a pretty tough conversation with one of my work friends, Sarah, about where I had been the previous week. I had messaged her the week before to say I wouldn't be in because I had an appointment, but I never specified what the appointment was for.

I then missed two more days that week, saying I was "ill"; this was an excuse I came to use a lot over the next few years.

I was helping Sarah with badminton lessons when she asked how the appointment went. I shrugged, and she asked what it was for. It took me a few minutes to respond; I wasn't sure if I wanted to tell her or not. However, I trusted her, so eventually explained where I had been, and followed it with a brief outline of what had happened. Then...

I am in his room. I can feel his hands on me. I try to scream but can't, I can only cry.

I managed to escape to the toilets to calm myself down. At this point, I had no idea how to deal with the flashbacks; I didn't even really know what they were, just that it felt as though it was happening all over again. That was the first time I remember punching a wall. I needed the images to leave my head, and both the pain and the shock helped with that.

Over the next few weeks, I had quite a few conversations with Sarah, and one in particular sticks in my head. I had already mentioned to her that I didn't know whether to report what had happened, and we'd gone over the pros and cons several times. This time, Sarah said to me, "What would you say to a friend if exactly the same thing had happened to them and they weren't sure what to do?"

That was when I knew I had to report it.

CHAPTER 5

INJUSTICE

At the time of writing, in the UK, only 1.4% of reported rapes in England and Wales result in a charge or summons.

The few months after the assault are mainly a blur, because all I could focus on was survival. I was on super high alert, 24 hours a day. Wherever I went or whoever I was with, I was constantly scanning, looking for danger. I couldn't switch off.

Although I decided to report the assault to the police, I completely understand why only around 15% of those who experience sexual violence choose to report it. The process is incredibly difficult. I found myself considering questions such as, "Will he do it again?", "Could I stop him before he does?", and "Can I deal with explaining all the details of that night to a complete stranger?"

I was also aware that anyone I had told about "that night" would have to speak to the police and repeat what I had told them, to ensure I had told people the same thing. Although I hadn't actually told many people – I was too ashamed.

At this point, I got the impression that my parents didn't want me to report it. I knew my dad had really liked Brad until this point, and had always encouraged me to hang out with him. I also think my mum was worried what reporting it would do to my mental health, as she could see I was already in a really bad place.

I knew deep down that I had to try to stop him from doing it again. And I realized that if I didn't report it, in the future I would regret it and wish that I had, especially if I ever found out he'd done it again.

If it wasn't for my ISVA, I would have definitely backed out of the initial video interview. I was TERRIFIED of having to relive the whole thing. And the process was, indeed, TERRIFYING. Some parts had to be repeated multiple times, for clarity, so that the detective could record every single detail, no matter how small. She asked the most intrusive, personal questions – things that I wouldn't discuss with people I had known for years! Yet, there I was, sitting in front of someone I had only just met, exposing my most personal of details. I had to – they needed to build their case. The worst part was that I knew there was a male officer in the next room, watching the whole thing on camera. Many other victims I have spoken to have said they didn't feel "believed", but thankfully for me, at this stage, this was not the case.

They had my clothes from that night already, but they took my phone as well, which made me feel like I was being investigated. I was just expected to buy a new phone. Surely, they should be taking his phone and interrogating him?

After the interview I didn't hear anything for a while. However, I was relaxed about it as I still had the text messages Brad had sent the day after, apologizing for what he had done, along with the messages he had also sent to my friend apologizing again.

Maybe a month or so later, I was in a car with two work friends when I received a phone call from the police telling me he had been arrested. That's when it hit me: he now knew I'd been to the police.

A few days later I got another phone call telling me he had been interviewed and released on bail. That absolutely terrified me. He knew where I lived, where I worked and went to university – was I safe?

After that, I heard nothing from the police for a few weeks, until they asked me to go back for some follow-up questions. Again, I was fairly relaxed given the evidence they had against him, although having to talk about it again was awful; but, with the help of my ISVA, I got through it.

Several weeks later I received a phone call while I was on the way home from work, and the detective dealing with my case told me he was coming to see me in half an hour to update me. I presumed this must be a good thing as I hadn't heard anything from them for a while. I asked the rest of my family to go out so we wouldn't be disturbed, but as soon as they did the anxiety started to build. I sat and waited at my parents' kitchen table, and the wait seemed like so much longer than half an hour.

I could tell immediately from the detective's facial expression that he didn't have good news. How stupid of me to presume it would be. He went through the usual formalities, and explained that they had so many similar cases and often there wasn't much evidence. They had to be able to prove what happened "beyond reasonable doubt", and without the evidence to do that he wouldn't be charged in court. He said it didn't mean they didn't believe me, just that a court wouldn't be able to prove it happened without a doubt. I knew what was coming.

He went on to tell me that they would be taking no further action. As I sat there it was like this fuzzy cloud filled my head. I couldn't think, let alone speak. How could they just drop it and not take any further action? The detective didn't hang about – he was obviously busy – but he suggested I get in contact with my ISVA as soon as I could. For a few minutes I couldn't move from the kitchen table. I felt completely let down and alone. Why had I bothered? The hours spent thinking through my decision, weighing up what I should do, and then the hours at the video interview. What had been the point? Then it happened again…

I was back in his kitchen. He was crying and threatening to stab himself with a massive kitchen knife. I thought he was going to turn it on me.

I understood the detective's point: if there wasn't enough evidence then the court would throw the case out, and as it's such a lengthy and often stressful process, it wouldn't be worth going through with it. So, part of me understood why they couldn't send it to the Crown Prosecution Service. What I didn't understand was how he'd wriggled his way out of the text messages he'd sent to me and my friend after "that night" in which he was clearly apologizing for what he had done. It was his word against mine.

He had won.

This was the worst possible news; it was a massive blow. It had taken so much courage to report the incident in the first place, and for it to be thrown back in my face because the evidence provided was argued to be "insufficient" was unbelievable. This was the first time I questioned if the police had ever believed me. How was I supposed to move on with my life? I was angry at the system. I was angry at the world.

CHAPTER 6

THE NEW NORMAL

The rest of university was tough. For the remainder of my first year, my attendance was terrible. When I did make the effort to turn up to a lecture, one of my parents would take me and wait for me. During the second year I mainly struggled in silence, because it was easier than explaining what was going on in my head; especially with this other "thing" that could not be spoken about messing with my head – there was no way I could explain that to anyone. My attendance continued to be ridiculously low, and I didn't socialize at all.

Some days, finishing university seemed pointless – the assault and the "thing" were never going away. And I saw everyone my age as a threat – men especially.

Often, I would leave seminars if the room was small and I wasn't near the door, as I felt trapped and would go into a complete panic. I had countless flashbacks and panic attacks in seminars throughout the rest of my time at university.

Some lectures weren't too bad: I got there, I listened and I left. However, seminars and practicals were often held in confined spaces, which was a different kettle of fish. Feeling trapped in a confined space would trigger flashbacks, and these were relentless. Group work or having to interact or discuss with my peers was a massive issue, given how threatened I felt. Similarly, the library and canteen were my worst nightmare – swarms of people my age, swarms of people just like him.

Before the attack, I'd been confident enough to speak in front of large groups, including one group of nearly 200 children at the summer camp I worked at; but now, being asked to talk or do a presentation in front of a few university classmates would throw me into absolute panic.

I avoided interacting with my peers as much as physically possible. My social life was non-existent because I didn't feel safe with people my age. At this point I didn't know I had post-traumatic stress disorder (PTSD), but looking back it's so obvious. I became more and more depressed, and most days I had zero motivation, and nothing mattered anymore.

Sometimes I struggled to motivate myself to write an assignment, or concentrate enough to put anything together. However, there were other days where assignments helped to distract me and gave me a focus.

I spent most of my time on edge – the smallest unexpected noise would panic me, and it was like my body was waiting for whatever bad thing was going to happen next. Even when my mind knew I was safe, my body didn't. The constant anxiety meant I struggled to eat, so I had even less energy.

My ISVA organized for me to have some counselling. While I know I had quite a few sessions, my memory of most of them are a complete blur. I was living in a constant state of fight or flight, which is why I think most of that period of my life is now so difficult to recollect – at the time it was hard to distinguish one day from the next.

One therapy session, however, is imprinted in my mind. My counsellor had picked up on the fact that I couldn't say the "r" word. We'd spoken about what had happened "that night" briefly, but it was apparent to her that I was in denial of the seriousness of that night. She had asked me to write down the definition of rape before the session, and I took it with me. I'd written it without much thought, and it wasn't until I got there that I really thought about it. It was during that session that it really hit me: that night, I had been raped. I still couldn't say it out loud though – and I wouldn't for a long time – but what happened next was progress, at least.

The counsellor asked me to write down "I was raped". It took me ages to do it, but, one letter at a time, I managed it.

That summer I found the confidence to sign up to work at a summer camp near York, which turned out to be an incredible experience. For seven weeks I was able to nearly completely forget about "normal life". It was like living in a bubble and, with limited internet access, was an escape from the world.

CHAPTER 7

OPENING UP

It was the first week of my final year of university. I was in a seminar, learning about the PE curriculum. I wasn't near the door, which was a huge error given how packed the room was. Only a few minutes in and it happened again…

I'm in his kitchen in my pyjamas and hoodie; he's got a knife. He's already locked the door and hidden the keys. I am trapped.

I couldn't stay in the room, so I did a runner. After punching something hard to try to bring myself out of the attack, I found myself pacing back and forth in a quiet corridor, away from the majority of students.

This pattern carried on for the next few months: I would either skip sessions, or I would attend and then leave when I had a flashback. I became more and more conscious of what everyone else on my course must have been thinking of me, and my mental health got worse and worse.

At the start of my final semester, in early 2018, a new lecturer, Ruth, started teaching at the university. In the second week of term, I missed her lecture. Everything had just got too much, and I couldn't face the world. I emailed Ruth with an excuse for my absence, and although I had never really spoken to her, she replied with something along the lines of, "If you need a chat, you know where I am."

I remember that week in particular; I was self-harming every day, I didn't want to be alive anymore. I felt that I couldn't tell anyone I was self-harming, as surely they'd think I was stupid. Cutting myself gave me a strange sort of relief that even now is hard to explain. It was so much easier to deal with the physical pain than the mental anguish. When you don't feel like you can talk about what's going on in your head and express how you're feeling, it feels like the only option. It was very much about control; I couldn't control the flashbacks and the nightmares. However, I could control the physical pain. It was a temporary release. But that was the thing, it was only temporary and it was a vicious cycle. I would self-harm to make myself feel better, but then I'd get really angry at myself, both for cutting and not coping more generally, and end up doing it again. Whilst self-harming made me feel better, it brought with it a whole host of other emotions; embarrassment, shame, and the knowledge that the scars might never fully disappear.

I'd been thinking about it for months, but a few days later I finally decided that I was going to crash my car on purpose. I knew that if I made sure I was going fast enough in my tiny car that I stood no chance. I was going to do it the following day on the way home from uni.

It was a Tuesday. We had Ruth's lecture in the morning, which I went to. I think she could tell I wasn't okay. I sat as far away from everyone else as I possibly could; I listened, but nothing really went in. Afterwards, I stayed behind to apologize again for missing the previous week's lecture, and to say thank you for her email. She asked me if I wanted to grab a brew and have a chat, and I realized then that if I didn't speak to someone, I was going to end up seriously hurting myself, or worse.

Until this point, I'd hardly told anyone about the PTSD – and I could count on one hand the number of people who knew the cause of it. We sat with a cup of tea for over an hour, and I told her everything. I'm not sure why, but I trusted Ruth instantly. I had never said, "I was raped" out loud until that day. That conversation saved my life, there is no doubt about it.

I know now that being able to admit "I was raped" was the first step to moving on. I will never forget what happened, it will never go away, and it is something I have to live with for the rest of my life. He stole something from me, physically and psychologically, which I'll never get back. In some ways, it would have been easier if he'd killed me. But this was definitely the first step in coming to accept what happened.

Even now, that conversation is one of the most therapeutic I've ever had. After speaking to Ruth, I went to see my GP, who put me on a waiting list for trauma therapy, and I hoped it wouldn't take too long.

A few weeks later I had my first appointment with Karen, a community psychiatric nurse. After an assessment, the plan was to start EMDR therapy (Eye Movement Desensitization and Reprocessing), but there was loads of preparation to do beforehand to make sure I was ready. We created a virtual toolbox in my head, with different coping mechanisms that I could turn to after I'd had a session.

I have since learnt that PTSD develops when the brain becomes overwhelmed with a traumatic event or a series of traumatic events and cannot process them correctly. This means the memories get stuck, or remain "unprocessed", and, as such, they can be continually triggered when you experience things similar to the difficult events you have been through. For me, seeing, smelling or hearing things related to the initial traumas could trigger a flashback or nightmare, or the feelings associated with them. For a long time these unprocessed memories were really affecting my ability to live in the present; the EMDR was intended to help with this.

EMDR involves reliving a traumatic or triggering experience in brief doses, while following either a light or your therapist's hands with your eyes, for me it was two lights on little handheld devices (like on a Nintendo Wii) which also vibrated. More often than not, our minds can heal themselves naturally, similarly to how the body does. Usually this happens when we are asleep, during the rapid eye movement phase.

EMDR aims to help the brain to process these memories properly, and files them away (as Karen described it) neatly, and in order. Over time, this meant my emotional responses to certain memories or thoughts would become less intense.

The cuppas with Ruth became a regular thing. I could speak to her about anything and everything. I am still so grateful for that initial chat, because it was the start of me being able to accept what had happened and begin to deal with it. I hate to think where I would have been without it. Ruth definitely got me through my final term of uni, and I'm certain I wouldn't have finished my course otherwise.

As soon as I'd handed in my final dissertation, I was going to escape to the Czech Republic as I needed to get as far away from my parents' house as I possibly could. When I returned to the UK to work at the summer camp again, that's when the EMDR would start.

CHAPTER 8

RUNNING

Two days after finishing university, I flew to the Czech Republic for a few weeks to work on an outdoor education programme with some friends, which was an absolutely amazing experience. We spent the days teaching kids how to build shelters, climb, and find their way around a town without speaking the language. The evenings were spent with a guitar and marshmallows round a campfire. One day we learnt about rivers and water purification in the middle of a forest, which was followed by lying in a hammock drinking tea we'd made from wildflowers, while my colleague read Dr. Seuss's *The Lorax* to the children. For the first time in years, I felt safe – as though I was untouchable, and nobody could hurt me again.

A few of us returned to England to work at Village Camps, like we had the previous summer. Just after we got back, the EMDR started, and it was tougher than I ever could have imagined.

Having to relive "that night" over and over again, while following two lights with my eyes so my brain would process the trauma properly, was horrendous; but it slowly got easier. It was made so much more bearable by working at the summer camp at the same time; I could distract myself afterwards, and lose myself in some random activity.

Over the course of the EMDR, the memories of this other "thing" from my childhood became more intense, and I started getting flickers of flashbacks from my childhood, of things I'd been working really hard to forget for a long time. I often woke up several times a night in a complete panic and covered in sweat from the nightmares, which then left me unable to sleep.

I was struggling to make sense of the memories of the events that I'd been trying to block out for years, but they slowly started to consume more and more of my headspace. I could never verbalize what was going on for me – it was way too scary to even think about admitting the stuff that was in my head.

That summer, aside from the EMDR, I had the most brilliant time. The staff at Village Camps became my extended family, and I truly felt like I fitted in, a feeling I wasn't used to. I made the most incredible friends from all over the world, but one girl in particular, Mailén, is still one of my best friends.

Over the course of the summer, Mailén and myself were offered more work in the Czech Republic during the autumn, so we decided to go on a road trip. It was the most incredible two weeks: camping, hiking, cooking on a tiny gas stove, driving for hours on the autobahn, swimming in rivers, drinking at beer festivals. We spent nights in London, Bruges, Antwerp, Ghent, Cologne, the Saxon Switzerland National Park and, finally, Prague, where we had the craziest night out in a super-sketchy underground club called (roughly translated) "Dog Bar". This underground bar had a discreet entrance, and once you were inside it was like something from a movie, with strange wooden benches and almost bunkbed-like furnishings. I'm not sure if it met any health and safety regulations: people were smoking all sorts, surrounded by candles and wood. After a trip to the bathroom I discovered how the bar got its name. I was very drunk, so I thought I was tripping, but I was in fact greeted by the biggest dog I have ever seen. It was way over half my size (admittedly that's not hard).

After recovering from the hangover, we headed south and worked in Vimperk for eight weeks, which again was just incredible. Cooking on campfires, teaching kids how to survive in the wild, and sleeping in hammocks in the middle of a forest. Over the course of these two months the flickers of flashbacks started to get more frequent, and more vivid; but it was easy enough to distract myself as I was surrounded by amazing friends and a beautiful national park. Mailén made me feel so safe – her confidence and ability to smile in any situation, whether we were lost and didn't understand the road signs, or if it was absolutely pouring down and the tent was leaking. However, I knew this had to come to an end and "normal life" had to resume at some point.

CHAPTER 9

ROCK BOTTOM

As soon as I got back to the UK, things went downhill.

I drove the long journey back to the UK on my own, over two days. As soon as I reached Yorkshire, I started feeling uneasy. My parents and sister didn't know which day I was coming home, and my brother was living down south at the time, so I had arranged for them all to be at the local pub with my aunty and uncle so I could surprise them.

Then, as soon as I stepped back into my parents' house, it happened…

I am 10 years old again and in my primary school uniform. We are in the woods in the village I live in. He is on top of me, I can't move.

Everything suddenly made sense. The snippets of flashbacks I'd been experiencing were suddenly pieced together. I thought I'd managed to run from this, but it looked like I couldn't anymore.

It had started when I was 10 years old. A family friend. A seemingly innocent game, which turned into something horrific. It went on for years, and only stopped when I was 14 and started "going out" with someone I had met on holiday in France. It was relentless, most of the "incidents" had no specific dates, so I couldn't remember exactly when they were. The exceptions were birthdays, Christmas and New Year, which were "special events", so the abuse was always worse. It is those occasions that are always stuck in my head.

Over the next few weeks I slowly slipped back into a deep depression, and I genuinely thought things would never get better. When I was a kid, I always thought depression was sadness, but it's far more complex than that. I know the depression was just one of the many symptoms of PTSD. It manifested itself as feelings of complete helplessness; waking up and lying in bed for hours and hours because I really couldn't see the point in getting up; feeling there was nothing waiting for me. I wasn't eating properly – again, what was the point? Sleeping was rare, and when I did sleep I was plagued with nightmares.

I had a few interviews for teacher training courses, which is what I had spent three years at university aiming towards, but it all seemed so pointless now. I even missed my own graduation. I started a new job, and then left again because I couldn't cope. I couldn't tell anyone what was going on. Partly because it still wasn't fully making sense in my head, partly because if I told anyone what was going on it became more real, and partly because I didn't know what other people would think. Would they blame me? Maybe I *was* to blame.

I had a week away in Lanzarote with my cousin, Courtney, which had been booked for ages and was a welcome escape; but as soon as I returned to England things became unbearable.

I knew I couldn't hide from it anymore, but at the same time I wasn't ready to face it.

The first time I got drunk to try to block out the memories was 18 November 2018; and then it became a regular occurrence. I knew the drinking was making things worse – the anxiety, the depression – but I needed it to get rid of the pain. Around the same time, I started self-harming again. Most of November and December of that year are pretty much a blur. I couldn't tell anyone what was going on, especially my family. What would they think? They'd want to know why I'd never told anyone. And they would have so many questions, which I was not in a fit state to deal with.

The flashbacks got worse and worse, and the anxiety at night was unreal. On the rare occasions I fell asleep, the nightmares were insufferable. I became afraid of sleeping, so I tried as hard as possible to not sleep. I spent most of my days watching random series on Netflix and trying to work out the best way to kill myself. I was now living with my cousin, Courtney. A few times I went back to my parents' to grab some clothes, but each time the reminders of the abuse made everything so much worse. On the last occasion I went to try to collect some clothes, it was too much; I had to pull over because I couldn't deal with the ongoing flashback. I turned round and went back to Courtney's. I realized I couldn't go back to the village I grew up in, and where my parents lived, because it was the place where so many bad things had happened.

I was gradually drinking and self-harming more and more, and I also started smoking weed to calm myself down. I felt like a boiling kettle, and I knew any day I was going to boil over.

CHAPTER 10

BOILING OVER

17 December 2018 was the day it boiled over, the day I got in the car and put my foot on the accelerator, the day of the near miss.

Going into the Crisis Cafe at Scarborough Survivors was one of the hardest things I've ever done. I sat in the corner with my hood up, and was brought a cup of tea by a lovely lady, who I now know is Val.

I answered some of their questions, of which there were quite a few, but I remember not feeling under pressure to tell them everything. It was a relief being able to admit that I wasn't okay and that I couldn't carry on the way I was. However, I wasn't honest about my living situation; I was in complete denial. They seemed to get it, and I instantly felt comfortable talking to a woman called Eileen. Eileen ended up being the first person I told about the abuse when I was a child, even though I didn't really tell her – rather I said something along the lines of, "some bad things happened when I was a child", so who knows what she thought. I stayed until the cafe closed at 1am, and because it had felt like a safe space, I knew I'd be going back.

Over the next few weeks I started going to Survivors more often. I went back to my parents a few times over Christmas, because doing that felt easier than telling my parents what was going on; but those visits made my mental health so much worse, to the point where I again started thinking about how I would kill myself.

At the Crisis Cafe, we made a "plan". I was going to get in touch with my GP, apply for Universal Credit, and try to get back in touch with Karen, the EMDR therapist. I was in the cafe, just doodling, when one of the volunteers, Carolyn, handed me an adult colouring book. It was so calming, and I spent many hours over the next few months colouring in to try to manage the anxiety. I also agreed to try to go into Survivors during the day, so I wasn't sitting around at Courtney's doing nothing. My drinking was becoming a real problem, and because I was only drinking to block out the awful memories and the feelings that came with them, there was no pleasure, only a slight numbing of the pain.

The next few weeks are mainly a blur, other than when I was in Survivors. The flashbacks and nightmares were worse than they had ever been, and they made me so, so angry. I was constantly lashing out, punching walls or other hard objects and seriously hurting myself.

It's hard to explain, but whenever I was in a really bad place or extremely overwhelmed, the pain and shock of any form of self-harm helped me, as dangerous as it was. Firstly, it was as though some of the mental pain was turned into physical pain, which was easier to deal with because it's tangible, not invisible. Secondly, the sudden pain and shock always brought me back into the present. I constantly had bruised and cut-up knuckles, and even ended up in Accident and Emergency a few times for X-rays.

I'm not sure what my family thought about why I wasn't living at home, or what they thought I was doing with my time; but I felt I couldn't tell them what was going on because I was so scared of their reaction.

CHAPTER 11

HOMELESS

At the beginning of January 2019, I realized I wouldn't be able to stay with my cousin much longer, and I had nowhere else to go – I was homeless. I still had my student bank account, but I'd managed to rack up over £1,000 on my overdraft, so I found myself applying for Universal Credit. Growing up, I had never expected that I would need to apply for benefits; but I think most people don't realize how easy it is to end up in a position where you need help, and even fewer people actually want to ask for help. It's mortifying, having to tell someone you've never met you're too mentally unwell to get a job, and that you have precisely minus £1,247 in your bank account.

If that wasn't bad enough, then having to go to a charity and tell them you don't have anywhere to live was truly humiliating. I was still in denial of my situation, and if it wasn't for the staff at Survivors I think I'd have buried my head in the sand for a bit longer. The local council wouldn't help me with my housing situation because I was under 25, so I was referred to another charity.

Around the same time, I visited my GP. I knew I wouldn't be able to verbalize what was going on, so I wrote it down. I passed her a note which said something along the lines of, "I was sexually abused as a child and I don't know how to deal with it". She couldn't have been more understanding. She asked me a lot of questions, mainly to assess how much of a risk I was to myself or anyone else, and, because I was a serious risk to myself, it ended with a referral to the crisis team until I could see Karen again.

However, the crisis team only made things worse. They always seemed to have someone in *more* of a crisis, or something else they had to deal with. Don't get me wrong, I understand they must be constantly busy, but making someone feel like you don't have time for them when they're already suicidal is not the answer. The first few days I answered their calls, they would ring and then make it very clear that they didn't have time for a real conversation, as if they were just trying to tick a box. So, I stopped answering as the phone calls seemed to make even not-so-bad nights really bad. On the nights that weren't as bad, by the time the phone call ended they were so much worse.

One night in particular, I was close to crashing my car again, so I pulled over and rang the crisis team, something I hadn't done before because usually I was too anxious to ring anyone. I was in complete despair – I didn't want to die. I had seen how good life can be, but I needed the pain to stop. I was told someone else was in crisis, and they would ring me back in ten minutes. When they did ring back, their advice was to have a bath and go to sleep. There was no compassion from their end, from supposed trained mental health professionals. PTSD stops you sleeping, but they had no time to listen, or even give appropriate advice, which looking back I think is horrific. It makes me wonder how many other people they fob off with ineffectual advice.

A few days later, I was back in Karen's clinic. My GP had passed on what I had told her, so I didn't have to explain again. She asked me a few questions, checked I hadn't done any serious damage with the self-harm, and then I managed to tell her a few details about what happened when I was a child. That's the first time I remember completely breaking down. By the end of the session, we had agreed I needed to see her again that week because I was in such a bad place. We also agreed that once I was more stable and less of a risk to myself, as well as in more permanent accommodation, we would restart the EDMR.

Over the next few weeks, I was seen by various people at local charities about my housing situation. They were pushing for me to find somewhere on SpareRoom.com, but I knew that mentally

I would not cope living with people I didn't know, or on my own because I was a danger to myself.

Around the same time, I also wrote my parents a letter telling them why I couldn't go back to their house. It was very brief, and I didn't give them any details, but I thought it was enough.

It got to the point where I had to leave my cousin's, I couldn't afford to contribute to any bills or pay for food, and I was increasingly feeling like I was in the way. That's when the reality of the situation hit me – I would have nowhere to sleep that night.

I contacted the charity I had spoken to previously and explained that my situation had changed. Not knowing where I would be staying was seriously scary, but I was lucky that, as I was under 25, I was entitled to emergency accommodation through Nightstop. It was a Friday, and I was told they would contact me late afternoon to let me know where I'd be staying. I didn't find out until 4pm where I was spending the night, and then I had to drive to Bridlington. Having to turn up at a stranger's house with all your belongings is awful, and I still struggle to find the words to explain that feeling even now.

The people I stayed with were lovely; they made me a really nice meal and, because it was a Friday night, I was supposed to be able to stay the whole weekend in the same place and go back to the charity on Monday. I was now drinking every day, and one of the rules of Nightstop is that you can't drink. I didn't want to risk getting kicked out, because I would literally be on the streets, but knowing I didn't have that crutch to get me through was challenging.

On the Saturday morning, the hosts got a call from one of their children, and they had to go down south immediately, meaning I had to leave. I packed my stuff up and headed back to Scarborough Survivors. I was now in the same position as the day before, not knowing where I'd be sleeping again. I found out before lunch where I would be staying that night, but spent the whole day dreading having to turn up somewhere new again. I stayed in the same place until Monday, but wasn't comfortable with it. It was close to where I lived growing up, which made me feel uneasy. It was also in the middle of nowhere, so I couldn't go to the Crisis Cafe in the evenings.

On Monday I was moved to a new place in Scarborough, where I was able to stay until Friday. The hosts, Sue and Bill, were so lovely; I felt like I could relax at their house, and I actually slept really well all week, for the first time in a long time. We had a really nice tea every night, and I was able to have a bath and spend the evenings reading. I didn't want to leave Sue and Bill's, but I was hopeful that the next place would be just as nice.

I saw my parents a few times that week, which was really nice but hard at the same time. After reading my letter they seemed shocked, and I don't think they could quite believe what I had told them. However, it wasn't something we spoke about and it was almost like the elephant in the room. All I wanted was to be able to go home with them; it wasn't their fault that I couldn't bring myself to do that, but I found myself getting really angry with them nonetheless.

I was told in advance that there was going to be a young man staying at my next placement, but there was nothing else available. This terrified me. I'd avoided men my age since university because they were significant triggers, but I knew I couldn't avoid them forever. I wasn't sure I was ready to stay in the same house as one.

But, I didn't have a choice. If I turned down the placement, I would have been without a roof over my head. I met the man later that night. He was quiet and we both loved football, which put my mind at ease slightly. I went to Survivors each evening, as usual. I knew that the time I was allowed to stay in Nightstop was coming to an end. You could only use Nightstop for two weeks, and then you should be placed somewhere more permanent. I didn't really know what my options would be after the two weeks were up, but on the Monday I had a phone call from the charity that runs Nightstop. They offered me a supported living placement, which was a similar concept to Nightstop, just longer term. It would mean staying where I had been in the final Nightstop placement. I was over the moon, and absolutely buzzing that I had a more permanent option, but I was still uneasy about staying with a man. I knew I had to start somewhere, and the charity also made it clear that there weren't any other placements available, so again I felt like I didn't have a choice. But I knew I always had Survivors during the days and evenings, so there was always somewhere else I could be for some of the time.

It was around this time that I met Leah. We came across each other briefly a few times in the Crisis Cafe. In the first few months of going to the cafe, I always sat in the corner with my hood up, not really speaking to anyone. As I got more comfortable, I started speaking to other people who were using the cafe. Leah and another girl called Jo were usually in Survivors at the same times I was, so we became pretty good friends and regularly ended up in McDonald's late at night together.

Leah and I soon realized we had a lot in common. When we met, we were both in seriously bad places, but our friendship helped each other get through some really tough times. We had both had bad experiences in childhood, and that pain connected us in a strange kind of way.

Leah, Jo and I nicknamed ourselves "The Three Musketeers", and between us there was always some sort of mischief. We had countless trips to Scarborough hospital and A&E over the following months, and I always felt like I was childminding two naughty schoolchildren when they would cause trouble in the hospital. The last time the three of us were all together, Leah and I were visiting Jo in hospital, and they thought it would be amusing to steal random objects from the nurses' station, and then even one of the beds!

CHAPTER 12

STABILITY

It felt strange staying in someone else's house. Looking back, I don't think I ever really settled in properly. The host was lovely, but it never felt like "home". Getting a hot meal every night was great, and I could always speak to either the host or someone from the charity if I needed to. My mental health was still pretty bad; the self-harm hadn't improved, and at times I still didn't want to be alive. The accommodation did provide me with some stability though; knowing where I would be sleeping each night removed the majority of the anxiety and uncertainty, which enabled me to start to work on a few things with Karen again.

The first thing we worked on was grounding myself after flashbacks and nightmares. Karen suggested I create a "grounding box", which has come to be one of the most useful tools in my recovery. The box contains quite a few items that would appear random if you didn't know the purpose of the box. It included a soft toy, lavender oil, fidget toys, photographs and letters from my best friends, and my favourite music – basically things that remind me I am safe. I still use it now, and the contents have grown to include literally anything that brings me back to the here and now.

Karen and I also started to work on my anxiety levels to try to help me sleep. We did a few different exercises but a particular favourite of mine was the "body scan". Body scanning involves paying attention to every part of the body in a gradual sequence, starting with the toes and finishing with the head. It allows you to check in with your body, because often physical discomfort can be linked to how we're feeling emotionally. The body scan always calmed me down. The main benefit was syncing my mind and body, as so often, especially after a nightmare or flashback, although my mind knew I was physically safe, my body would react as if I was not. The body scan would bring me into the present.

I was seeing my parents fairly frequently now, but I found myself getting so angry with them, and with the whole situation more generally. I didn't understand how no one could not have noticed what was going on when I was a child. What did they think was happening when I stopped doing my homework and started misbehaving at primary school, or when I smashed my bedroom up? How did no one notice when my behaviour changed so much? I didn't blame my parents, but I had so many unresolved things whizzing round my head at the same time and I didn't know how to cope with these questions.

Around the same time, I started to think about reporting the childhood abuse to the police. However, my previous experience of the reporting process completely put me off. I also knew that I would have to verbalize everything – every tiny, painful detail – which I was not ready to do. But at least I knew going to the police was an option.

I continued going to Survivors most days, and even though most people were a lot older than me, I found it really calming and started to make friends. My days were all pretty much the same though, and I noticed I was stuck in repeated patterns. I knew that to stop my mental health getting even worse I had to try to switch things up and make some changes. I came across an advert on Twitter at the end of February for a new sporting programme called Get on Track, run by the Dame Kelly Holmes Trust and North Yorkshire Sport. The idea was to improve the mental health of young people using physical activity, which sounded perfect for me.

The first few days of the course were pretty nerve-racking, because it was the first time since university that I had been around so many people of a similar age to me, which was a huge challenge. There was also a lot of arguing among the participants in the first week. Most of the other young people on the course lived in the hostel in town, and

I got the impression it was tough for them being around each other 24 hours a day. Quite a few of them spoke openly about the drugs they'd been taking the night before, so the come-downs probably explained the combative behaviour. As a result, only a few of us turned up the following week, and the atmosphere was much calmer. We also had more time with the athlete mentors to talk about what was going on for us, and why we'd signed up to the programme. The mentors, Jody, James, Paul and Ian, were all really understanding and always happy to talk if one of us was having a particularly bad day. They got us speaking in front of each other, debating, and really pushed us out of our comfort zones.

Over the course of a few weeks, we went mountain biking, climbing and played rugby on the beach. I'd always known how much being physically active helped me, but like many people I struggled to motivate myself when my mental health was bad. I'd played and loved football since the age of five, sometimes at quite a high level, but since "that night" in 2016, I hadn't been able to face it; I'd stopped playing and even watching football completely. I'd met Brad through a football scholarship at college, and our entire friendship was based around football. We went to see each other play, went to games together and watched our favourite teams on TV together. It really hurt me knowing I was giving up the one thing that had always kept me sane, but whenever I tried to get back to football, I couldn't deal with the aftermath. Brad had always encouraged me to play, to push myself and to go for trials; so, as daft as it sounds, I felt like I had to stop, because he would have hated me stopping. For such a long time I couldn't even watch it, let alone play. I know now that not playing is letting him control another aspect of my life – but that's something I've still got to work on.

CHAPTER 13

EMDR, ROUND 2

Towards the end of March 2019, Karen and I decided it would be a good time to restart the EMDR therapy. My mental health had become more stable than it had been for a while, and although I knew it would be a really tough process, I also knew it would benefit me in the long run. It's hard to put into words the sheer terror of having to finally face up to, and, even worse, verbalize things that I'd spent so long running from. Over the course of the next few months, I spent countless hours focusing back and forth on two flashing lights, while replaying my most painful memories.

The first time I had tried EMDR therapy, I had been extremely sceptical. However, I felt like I was seeing the benefits, and the memories of "that night" seemed to become slightly easier to deal with – the nightmares and flashbacks became slightly less intense, and I found it easier to relax.

I remember the first session of my second round of EMDR specifically, mainly because it was so hard. Karen asked me to pick one of the memories from my childhood to work on first. As I'd done previously, I would talk her through it, slowly. I had so many awful memories constantly buzzing round my mind, but I chose one that had been particularly playing on my mind…

We are in the woods in the village where we live. I am in my primary school uniform. He is on top of me, and I have no clue what is going on. I am crying. Everything hurts.

I think many people don't realize that PTSD is not just your brain remembering trauma, but your body is remembering too. With flashbacks and nightmares, it's like the events are physically happening all over again. You're back there, you're not safe. The rational part of your brain knows you are safe, but the irrational side of it, along with your body, doesn't. So, as I was sitting there in that room with Karen, in my mind I was back there. I could *feel* everything, as if it was happening in that moment.

After a few moments of silence, Karen said something and I was brought back to where I was, and that I was, in fact, safe. She asked me again to talk her through that particular memory. Even though it was still very much at the forefront of my mind – I couldn't not think about it, even if I tried – and even though I focused all my energy on trying to say the words, I just couldn't. I'm not sure if it was the shame, or the fear of it all becoming so much more real once I'd said it out loud, that stopped me.

It soon became apparent that I physically couldn't get the words out. Luckily, Karen had a plan B (she always did!). She suggested that, before the next session, I write down all of the different memories I had of the abuse, and then I might find it easier to read one out. I knew that even writing them down would be incredibly hard, but surely it had to be the easier option.

EMDR therapy can still be effective without talking through things, just using the images, but even that is tough and mentally exhausting. The rest of the session was spent trying to bring me back to the present, so I could leave in a relatively "okay" frame of mind.

EMDR therapy is exhausting, and whenever I had sessions, I always spent at least the next few days absolutely shattered and not wanting to do much. I would normally leave in a "not-too-bad" headspace, but by the time I'd either driven or taken the train home and had time in my own head, I was usually in a completely different place.

The following night, at the Crisis Cafe, I set about trying to do my "homework".

I was still in a pretty bad shape from the therapy session, so I went and sat in the corner with my hood up; I didn't want to speak to anyone. Eileen came over, and, after my usual "I feel like shit" responses, she got out of me what was going on. It made it easier having Eileen, Christie and Leah there while I worked on my memories. After a few hours, and several flashbacks, I had written down every single incident I could remember. Luckily, Leah was there for me when I finished with a packet of cigarettes and a hug. Smoking the cigarette in relief, I realized how much I'd achieved just by writing it all down. This was the first step, and although I knew I still had a long way to go, the feeling of accomplishment gave me my first small glimmer of hope.

CHAPTER 14

FIRST STEPS

Throughout March and April 2019, all of the young people living in the supported living scheme in Scarborough were invited to a number of different events, including a theatre visit and a trip to Inflata Nation, and to several workshops, one of which was on LGBT awareness, run by Yorkshire MESMAC (a sexual health organization). Honestly, I didn't want to go. I thought that, because I was openly gay, it was slightly pointless; but I was at the charities' office anyway for an appointment with my support worker, so decided to stay on.

Just before it started, I met Lilly who was running the session, and I instantly loved her vibe. She told me about the LGBTQ youth group they ran, and mentioned I could join it as a young person or as a volunteer. We arranged to have a chat the following week at the office, and I eventually decided I would go along to get a feel for it.

Other than Survivors and seeing Leah, I wasn't socializing. I'd been avoiding the friends I used to spend a lot of my time with as I knew they would ask awkward questions about where I was living, where I was working, what I was doing with myself, and why I wasn't living with my parents anymore. I didn't want to lie to them, but I knew they would see straight through me, especially my old friend Sarah. I thought the youth group would be a good place to start on reviving my social skills, and Lilly seemed to get me.

I really enjoyed the group, and I decided I would become a volunteer as the kids were quite a bit younger than me. It was good knowing that one evening a week I had a purpose that was really important. I could focus on something other than the thoughts in my head, which was really helpful, even if it wasn't for long.

I knew Lilly would never judge me, even though she was constantly pushing me out of my comfort zone, which I needed. We had regular cuppas, and I knew I could speak to her about anything. I ended up volunteering at both York Pride and Harrogate Pride, which again pushed me out of my comfort zone and forced me to speak to new people, which turned out to be great for my confidence.

One of the things I love about Lilly is that she is always brutally honest with me – she tells it how it is, and that's always something I will be so grateful for.

CHAPTER 15

SURF THERAPY

At the beginning of May 2019, I had a completely random phone call from the housing charity that had got me the initial place in Nightstop. An organization was setting up a new surf therapy scheme, and they thought I would be the ideal candidate. Surfing was something I had always wanted to try, especially since I'd moved to Scarborough, but I'd never had the opportunity to do so. I went for the assessment and agreed to give it a go – I knew it couldn't make things any worse.

The first session was on 22 May, and although I was really excited, the anxiety was overwhelming. What if I drowned? What if I was the only girl? The anxiety got the better of me, and I didn't show up, but I instantly regretted not going. I texted the lady who had been at my assessment and she offered to pick me up the following week, so I wouldn't have to arrive alone, which definitely helped.

I joined the group – again with my hood up, which was my anxiety default as it stopped me having to make eye contact with anyone. I was introduced to the instructors and the other participant, Phil, and given a wetsuit to put on. We carried the boards down to the beach and then sat while Matt and the other instructor gave us a quick overview of technique. Most of what he said didn't go in because I was panicking too much to concentrate. There were quite a few people on the beach, so as usual I was on high alert, scanning for potential danger.

Once I was in the sea, the strangest thing happened. It was as though all of my anxiety just disappeared, something that had never happened before. As soon as I caught that first wave, that was it, I was hooked. The feeling of riding the wave was something else completely, and even before I even tried to stand up on the board, the sense of freedom was unreal. It wasn't until the second session that I attempted to stand up, which was an even better feeling. Before I knew it, I was surfing twice a week, and then nearly every day over the summer. Even on days when there were no waves, I would borrow a board and paddle out just to get that sense of calm that the sea brought with it. I knew that whenever I was in the water, all my problems – the flashbacks, nightmares, anxiety and fear – would disappear for a few hours, and I could be a completely different, chilled-out person.

The hours I spent in the water were my form of mindfulness. When you're surfing you can't afford to think about anything else, because if you lose focus for even a few minutes you can end up swept out in a rip, colliding with another surfer, or on top of a reef. Even when you have a "bad surf", it's still a complete distraction. It gave me a focus, something to aim towards. When you're up against something as powerful as the sea, it's a huge challenge, and even when you're getting absolutely pummeled by the waves it makes you feel like you're really achieving something.

There were quite a few surf sessions where the other participants didn't turn up, so I had one-on-one lessons with Matt. I'm truly grateful that, even when I turned up in the worst mood possible, quiet and withdrawn, he didn't give up on me. He persevered with talking to me and getting me to communicate; he taught me about beach safety, rips, how the weather affected the surf, marine life, and so many other interesting things. I think he knew that by teaching me about the surf environment, which I found extremely cool, it would get me out of my own head. When I started surfing, I had no confidence in the water and panicked if I went out of my depth. Matt taught me how to get out of a rip, helped me improve my swimming, and just generally believed in me when I didn't believe in myself.

CHAPTER 16

"INTENTIONALLY HOMELESS"

A few months after I moved into the supported living placement, I was made aware that the host would be having some exchange students to stay. Apparently, she did it every year, but no one had warned me when I moved in. Usually, the students were male and of a similar age to me. The charity that had placed me there knew my background, and how male-specific my PTSD is, especially when they are of a similar age to me.

I made the charity aware early on that I wasn't comfortable with the situation, and stayed out of the house as much as possible when I knew there would be males there. I was already living with one, who I was slowly getting more comfortable with. The charity made it clear that there were no other placements available, so I had to stay put. For a while, I stuck with it and either stayed with my cousin when I knew people would be at my placement, or stayed at Survivors or with Leah until late into the night.

It came to a head when even more young men were scheduled to stay. One was coming for a longer-term placement to learn English, and then a group of four were staying just for a week. Again, I made it very clear to the charity that I wouldn't be able to deal with staying in the same house (a small house with one bathroom!) with a total of six young men. I knew I had to work through my issues with men, but that was something I had to do gradually and over time, with the help of therapy. Nevertheless, I was told on several occasions, by both workers from the charity and my host, that it was something I just had to "get over", and this sort of exposure was the only way I'd overcome my fears. I remember my housing worker telling me over and over again that, "Not all men are bad". Obviously, I knew that because some of my friends are male, but to this day I still question her complete lack of understanding and knowledge about the effects of trauma, especially when she was working with so many young people affected by different types of trauma. When you've been abused by men, they become a trigger, especially when you develop PTSD. I never argued with the "not all men are bad" argument at the time, because I was in such a bad place that forming a coherent counter-argument was never one of my priorities. Looking back, I wish I had stuck up for myself, and countered the complete disregard and lack of understanding shown by supposed "professionals". I understand that the charity was stretched and had limited placements, but no one who has experienced trauma should ever be told to "get over it".

There's so much talk these days about "trauma-informed care" and "physiologically informed environments", and they are vitally important issues. When I speak at events or to professionals, I always use the previous example. And I will never understand how someone in the support sector can say, on countless occasions, to a young female who has experienced abuse at the hands of men that "not all men are bad".

Anyway, I was told there were no other placements available. I approached another charity, to ask about spaces in their hostel. I was told I wouldn't be top priority because I currently had somewhere to live, so there would be a long wait. I explained that although the placement I was in may be considered physically safe, it wasn't psychologically safe, and my mental health was deteriorating very quickly. The nightmares and flashbacks were intensifying, the self-harm was increasing in both frequency and severity, and I was getting to the point where I wanted to end it all. Yet I was told, loudly and clearly, that if I left my current placement, I would be making myself "intentionally homeless" and, as such, would not be entitled to *any* help.

I had signed a tenancy agreement when I moved in to my placement, which committed me to staying there at least four nights a week, and I always had to let the host know if I would be staying elsewhere. But I started doing my own thing, staying out all week and not letting them know where I was. My opinion was: they wouldn't listen to me and be considerate of my PTSD, so why should I follow their rules?

After the bigger group of young men arrived things really got bad. Once, I went back briefly to get changed before going to Survivors and three of them were in the (very small) kitchen, meaning I had to squeeze past them...

I am stuck in his kitchen. Locked in and unable to find the keys; panicking.

I left the house as fast as I could and ran down the street in a complete panic. I couldn't deal with it, and I couldn't deal with the fact that no one was listening to me or thinking about what I needed. The anger took over, and I spent the next few minutes repeatedly punching a wall. It was almost an automatic reaction. It hurt, but I needed a way of getting the anger out, and I didn't know how else to do it.

That was when I knew I couldn't go back. I knew I had to look after my mental health before it deteriorated past the point of being able to help myself. Even if the charity wasn't taking it seriously, I had to look out for myself.

CHAPTER 17

REPORTING, ROUND 2

During my sessions with Karen, and as the EMDR therapy progressed, I started to become more able to verbalize the things that had happened to me as a child. And I came to the realization that I couldn't *not* report the abuse I experienced during my childhood. What would I do if I found out he'd, in the future, done the same things to someone else, and I could have prevented it?

I knew I still wasn't quite ready to do it, because I still couldn't even say most of the stuff that had happened to me out loud. I was also completely put off by my experience of reporting the last time around, and didn't have any belief in the criminal justice system.

A few weeks later, Leah became unwell, and while she was inside her flat talking to a paramedic and a police officer, I waited outside with another police officer. We were talking about Survivors and what I wanted to do with my life, which I didn't really have an answer for at that point. I did know, however, that, in some way, I wanted to help other people who found themselves in similar situations to me. We spoke about how I'd wanted to be a police officer when I was younger, and they said I still could be, but I pointed out that already being diagnosed with PTSD probably wasn't part of the job description. We discussed PTSD, how I dealt with it, and how much Survivors had helped me along with what caused it. The big question then was, "Have you reported that to the police?" I sheepishly explained that I hadn't, but that I had been thinking about it, and just wasn't sure I'd physically be able to go through with it. By the end of the conversation, I knew I had to act. They booked me an appointment at the police station the following week to sit down with an officer and give them a few more details. I think that without that conversation I would have kept putting it off, telling myself I couldn't go through with it.

After a few days, I started to panic. What if the words physically wouldn't come out? What if they didn't believe me? What if I went through the trauma of saying it all out loud and it turned out to be for nothing? I wanted to cancel the appointment. I was going to cancel the appointment.

A few days later I set off to Survivors, which meant walking through the town centre. I bumped into two PCSOs, Karen and Donna, who I'd met a few times previously when I'd been hanging out with Leah. I explained briefly to Karen that I had this appointment at the police station the following week which I wanted to cancel, but I was too anxious to ring up and cancel it. They offered to walk up to the police station with me, and as we walked I tried to explain why I couldn't go through with it. Karen explained how it would work and tried to reassure me, although I still wasn't convinced. By the time we'd reached the police station, she had almost convinced me just to go for that initial chat, and then see how I felt and reassess. I think she could tell how terrified I was, and what she said next really changed things for me. "If you want, I will meet you here ten minutes before the appointment, if it makes you less anxious?" I was very grateful, and agreed to go for the initial chat, on the condition that it would be a female officer.

They walked me back to Survivors, and reassured me that I only had to say as much as I was comfortable with at the initial appointment. I was still terrified, but it was comforting that I wouldn't have to go alone.

By the time the day of the appointment came, I hadn't slept for more than two hours at a time for five days. I felt sick with anxiety, and if it wasn't for the fact that I was too anxious to ring up and cancel the appointment, I would have bottled it.

Scarborough Police Station isn't the most welcoming of places, even on a good day. The four plastic chairs in the entrance reminded me of being at school, and I felt like I was about to be interrogated.

I'd stressed that it needed to be a female officer (for obvious reasons) when I made the appointment, and again when I'd spoken to them with Karen the PCSO. But the officer who came to get me was male. The panic completely took over, I couldn't even stand up. Karen asked if I was okay. All I could get out was, "It needs to be female". The officer said there were no females on duty. I was ready to run. Karen offered to stay with me if it meant I would speak to them, to which I nervously agreed.

I don't remember most of the appointment, but I do remember crying. I hadn't cried for such a long time, and it seemed to be an emotion that I had managed to turn off. I think the poor officer felt very awkward. But what did he expect? He knew why I was there, and he knew I'd requested a female officer. How did he think I felt? He went to get a female colleague and returned with someone from CID. We were there for over two hours, and I'm fairly certain most of it was spent in silence, with me struggling to get the words out. I cannot express how much it meant to me that Karen offered to stay with me, because I know that was a positive step in my healing journey. If I hadn't gone through with it, who knows where I would be now.

A few weeks later, I met with two detectives in the park outside Survivors so they could talk me through the whole process again. I also thought meeting them would make me slightly more comfortable with going through with the video interview.

A detective was assigned to the case, and he contacted me several times over the next few weeks to try to get me to make an appointment for the video interview. I kept putting it off; I didn't think I could go through with it.

Eventually he rang while I was at Survivors and – after a conversation with Eileen and Christie, who offered to come to the video interview with me – I agreed to a date a few weeks later.

The week before the video interview, the female detective picked me up from surfing and took me to the house where the video interview would be conducted, so I could get a feel for the place and know what to expect. It was very similar to where I had undertaken the video recording for the sexual assault a few years before – it was a house with a living room, kitchen and bathroom, and then another living room where the interview would take place. There were cameras and microphones recording, but you couldn't tell. I still didn't feel ready, but I knew I never would, and at some point, I had to take the leap.

CHAPTER 18

FEAR

As I hadn't been able to return to my supported living placement, I had been staying with my cousin again for a few weeks until there was another option. So, when the day of the video interview arrived it meant things were even more scary and chaotic. On Friday 21 June 2019, I met Eileen outside Scarborough Police Station at 1:50pm, ten minutes before we needed to be there. I was shaking, I felt sick, and I genuinely didn't think I could get through the rest of the day.

But everything is slightly easier when you've got someone like Eileen by your side. I don't think she gets enough credit for everything she's done, not just for me, but for so many other people I know.

Once we arrived at the house, the detective made me a brew and went over how the interview would work. Leah had given me a cuddly toy to take with me because she knew how terrified I was. As I sat there, filled with sheer panic at what was to come and gripping this cuddly toy, I felt like a small child again – completely helpless.

I had spent years trying to remove the images and thoughts from my childhood from my head; but now I had to face up to them. I had to think about them and, even worse, verbalize them. If you've never been through the process of reporting sexual violence, you won't realize the level of detail you have to go into – every little thing matters. It feels strange because, for me, the bad stuff happened so many years ago, yet all the memories are so clear, as if it happened yesterday. That's the thing about PTSD, every time you have a flashback or nightmare it's like it's happening all over again – you can't forget.

After an hour and a half, I think the detective realized it was getting too much for me. We took a tea break. It was like time was going really fast, but it had stopped at the same time. Once I had started talking, some of it just came out without me having to think about it, until I got to the most difficult memories. There was one in particular that was causing me the most distress. I hadn't even told my therapist Karen about it yet, because I'd realized I couldn't even write it down, let alone say it out loud. I went through some of the other memories first, saving that one until I was feeling slightly braver.

Once we'd been there for three hours the detective said we were going to stop for the day and come back next week. That's when I lost it. I'd got it in my head that, after that day, it would be over, I wouldn't have to speak about it again – but, no, I had to go back the following week, with the worst of the memories still to go. We went back into the room where Eileen was waiting, and I don't think I've ever cried so much. It was like all of the memories were playing in my head, on a loop with no off switch.

We got in the car and I noticed they drove us back to Scarborough the long way round, probably to try to calm me down before dropping us off. I was so exhausted, both physically and emotionally, that I could have fallen asleep in the car. They dropped us off and Eileen took me for fish and chips, followed by a long walk along the sea front to refresh me. I was physically and emotionally exhausted, but my mind wouldn't switch off. We got to Survivors early, so I set about trying to do some colouring to distract myself.

For hours the flashbacks were non-stop, and I got myself incredibly wound up and exhausted. I felt like a scared child again, sitting there with my cuddly toy for comfort. Being able to sit with Eileen, Christie and Leah helped no end, and made me feel physically safe while my mind was making me feel ridiculously unsafe.

That weekend was tough. The exhaustion coupled with not being able to sleep meant I was an absolute mess, and I knew the worst of it was still to come. There was no relief.

The following Friday, I met Eileen again outside the police station. Although I felt slightly more prepared, I was still terrified at verbalizing that one specific memory. I also knew for sure that after that day it would be over and done with, which helped slightly. We went through the same routine: the detective made me a brew and we headed into the interview room. I'd been practising talking through that one specific memory all week, but I still didn't think I'd be able to go through with it. How do you tell someone that the worst thing that could possibly be done to a person, was done to you?

We were in there for another three hours, with a break halfway through; and I have no idea how I got through it. I cried for most of the second half of the interview, and once we were finished, I completely broke down again. As they had the previous week, the detectives drove us the long way back to town. Eileen got us a McDonald's, and we headed straight to Survivors. I knew it was over, but the flashbacks were still non-stop.

The weekend following the interview was tough, but I managed to surf with one of my friends, which gave me a brief reprieve from the flashbacks.

CHAPTER 19

NIGHTSTOP

A few days after the interview I was back in the position of not having anywhere to sleep. I had been told I wouldn't be entitled to any emergency accommodation because, by leaving my placement, I was making myself intentionally homeless. But I got extremely lucky, because one of the mentors at the surf therapy programme happened to know someone who worked for one of the housing charities, and was able to get me back into Nightstop. Although the anxiety returned as I didn't know exactly where I would be sleeping that night, I knew it had to be better than where I had been.

The anxiety subsided as soon as I got a phone call to say I could stay with Sue and Bill again, which I was extremely grateful for. And I was able to stay there until a room became available in the hostel in town, which I was now a priority for. I stayed for two weeks.

Around the same time, Leah was admitted to hospital. We weren't exactly sure what was wrong with her, but they told us she'd have to stay for a few weeks. I visited her as often as I could, took her clothes and chocolate, and we got up to plenty of mischief around the hospital.

On 14 July 2019, two weeks after she had gone into hospital, I was told indirectly that Leah had been given 48 hours to live. I didn't believe it at first, but a message from her mum confirmed it was true. Her liver had failed, she'd developed pneumonia and sepsis, and there was nothing they could do for her. I got to York Hospital as fast as I could, and I thought it might be the last time I saw her.

The following day I was told she had been moved to intensive care, and that only family could visit. I was absolutely heartbroken; she was the only person who really understood me.

Two days later, I received a phone call telling me I could move into the hostel that same day. I also found out that Leah had improved slightly, and because she was now awake and was asking for me, I could visit her in intensive care. That gave me hope that maybe she would defy the odds and get better.

She was a fighter, after all.

CHAPTER 20

HOSTEL

On 16 July 2019, after seeing Leah, I moved into the hostel in Scarborough. I was nervous about moving in, because I'd heard so many bad stories about it from other people, and I'd been warned about the partying. As soon as I moved in, I was reintroduced to some of the individuals I had met on the Get on Track course earlier in the year. I got on well enough with them, and I was quickly invited to hang out with them, which at the time I was grateful for, and I wanted to fit in.

I met a few of the staff during the first few days and they were all lovely, but I got on particularly well with Lisa, who just seemed to "get me".

My sleeping was still terrible, and most days I was awake by 7am after no more than a few hours of sleep. The hostel provided a free breakfast before 10:30am on weekdays, to encourage us to get up and do something with our days. The kitchen opened at 8:30am, and I think the staff were pretty shocked to see me in there as soon as it opened – I don't think they were used to early risers.

I hadn't touched weed since I had started going to Survivors, but within two days of moving into the hostel I was smoking it again as a result of hanging out with a girl called Georgina. It did help me sleep though, and while I know the sleep wasn't the same quality as "proper sleep", it was a welcome relief from the PTSD that had been keeping me awake. It didn't take me long to start dabbling in other drugs, which is something that I have not admitted to many people until writing this book. I guess I was ashamed that it was the only thing that seemed to help, and ashamed that I didn't have more effective ways of dealing with the stuff that was going on in my head.

But the weed really messed with my head, too. When I only had one joint I could go back to the hostel and sleep for a good few hours. It quickly became more than a one-joint affair though, and we would spend hours getting stoned. I didn't know when to stop, and I lost all ability to say "No". I would keep going and going until I was seeing things that weren't there, I would get intrusive thoughts telling me to kill myself, and my anxiety went through the roof.

I spoke to Lisa about most things, and we would spend Monday evenings and Sundays playing pool on the hostel's mini pool table, playing card games and watching soaps. I knew she'd never judge me or tell me what to do.

CHAPTER 21

LEAH

It turned out that 16 July would be the last time I saw Leah. I wasn't able to visit again because she deteriorated and visiting became for family only. She survived for nearly three more weeks (I told you she was a fighter). The last time I saw her she was winding the doctors and nurses up – she never lost her sense of humour. She died on 5 August, and, even though I knew it was coming, it completely broke me. I was so angry at the world – why did such a nice, caring person have to go through so much trauma and then not be given the help to deal with it, despite years of asking? Why were so many good people being failed by the system?

I found out she'd died from a post on Facebook. I was absolutely heartbroken. She was the one person who I knew understood me, and she was gone. Luckily, Lisa was on shift when I found out and we were able to go for a walk. I couldn't face seeing the other young people in the hostel. Lisa and the security guard who was working at the hostel that night had also both known Leah, which helped. We spent most of that night drinking tea and playing pool.

The funeral was the following week, and Leah would have loved it. The dress code was Nike Airs with purple, and Leah's famous luminous pink trainers were on top of the casket. They played Rihanna's "Diamonds" and finished the service off with "Bonkers" by Dizzee Rascal, one of Leah's favourite songs. It was a hard day, but I knew Leah was no longer in pain and she didn't have to face up to the things she'd spent so long running from, and drinking to avoid. But... man, I bloody missed her.

CHAPTER 22

PEER PRESSURE

The longer I stayed in the hostel, the worse the drug situation became; one day in particular, a big group of us started smoking weed in the early evening and continued to smoke constantly for a good few hours. There was a no-drugs policy in the hostel, but no one took any notice. At some point the smoke alarm started going off, and there was a delay of a few minutes before the whole building's fire alarm was triggered. That day the staff member that was on duty from 5pm to 9pm had called in sick, so although the hostel stank of weed, no one was there to stop the drug taking. That night, I ended up walking around Scarborough, completely out of it, until well past 1am, with the intention of killing myself. Eventually, the drugs wore off, I realized the time and went back to the hostel.

If you were caught with drugs on you in the hostel, or smoking weed in your room, you got a warning; but as soon as the staff left at 9pm the fun began. When I first moved in it was mainly weed, but within a few months everyone was taking Class A drugs.

I knew I didn't want to be taking drugs, but at the same time I didn't know how else to deal with the stuff that was going on in my head. And the peer pressure was immense – I struggled to say "No" to the people I was living with, especially Georgina.

Whenever Lisa was on shift, I didn't feel like I had to join in, as I would be playing pool or cards, or watching soaps. I remember speaking to Lisa about the fact I was struggling with the peer pressure. She gave me a bit of a pep talk, and then Georgina came into the kitchen to ask if I was going "out", which actually meant going on a drug pick-up. I took on board Lisa's advice, and said, "No, sorry, I'm busy," for the first time. Once Georgina had left, Lisa told me she was proud of me, which meant a lot. I think she realized how much it had taken to say no to someone like Georgina, but after that things were never great between me and Georgina.

Over the next few weeks I continued to struggle with saying no to the young people I was living with, especially Georgina. She had a way of making you feel small and insignificant, and if you didn't get involved with the drugs, you were automatically excluded from hanging out with them. I knew the drugs made me feel better for a little while, but I also knew they made me feel much worse in the longer term. I needed the escape, but I didn't need the come-down and anxiety that it brought with it. I was still giving in to the peer pressure and I caved under duress, but I always woke up regretting it.

One night, after failing to opt out, I turned up to Survivors high, knowing full well that I wouldn't be allowed in because I wasn't sober. I just wanted to let them know I was okay, because I hadn't seen them in a few days. Thankfully, as there was no one else in the building, they let me in. I had smoked way too much, to the point that I really wanted to hurt myself. But being around Eileen and Christie helped me calm down, even though when I got back to the hostel I was still ridiculously on edge.

The next day, someone I respected told me about the potential of certain drugs triggering hallucinations because I was suffering with PTSD. The thought of this really scared me, so I vowed to stop.

Despite the drug taking, there were many positives to the hostel that helped my mental health. There were staff there until 9pm every night, and then security guards overnight, and I already knew one of the security guards because he had worked where Leah lived. Knowing there was someone there 24 hours a day made me feel safer, and I knew (depending on which staff member it was) that there was usually someone I could speak to if things got bad. There were also scheduled activities, such as cooking, movie nights and occasional outings.

Around a month after I moved in, so did a girl called Amber, and we got on instantly. We spent hours watching the TV show *Criminal Minds*, playing pool and drinking unhealthy amounts of tea.

Not long after moving in, one of the hostel's "move-on" flats became available. I was offered it, but I knew I wasn't ready. I was still finding the EMDR therapy extremely tough. I knew I wasn't through the worst of it, and, with the police case still ongoing, I needed the level of support that the hostel offered me. The manager at the hostel agreed I could stay until just after Christmas, when the therapy would be finished and we would know more about the police investigation. I had also told them I would struggle at Christmas time because on special occasions, such as Christmas, New Year and birthdays, the abuse was always worse, meaning so too was the PTSD. I knew I was going to need the security the hostel offered.

Towards the end of the summer, I started doing a jigsaw that I found in the hostel. It was 1,000 pieces and different staff members and residents would help me when they were in the kitchen. Between us, we finished it within a week, and I started on another one. I spent hours at the jigsaw table, and was able to use the puzzle as my excuse not to do drugs: I was too busy, obviously. Regularly being able to say no to the drugs meant my mental health started to improve, but it didn't do me any favours in the hostel.

Georgina could be particularly volatile when she wanted to be; but I realize she was dealing with her own stuff, in her own way, so I don't blame her at all. One Thursday, I returned from my EMDR session and headed for the kitchen for a brew and to crack on with my jigsaw with Amber. We had the TV on so we could continue binge-watching *Prison Break*. Georgina came in, banging and shouting. As usual, following the EMDR session I was in a bad place – anxious, more on edge than usual, and extra sensitive to loud or sudden noises. I politely asked Georgina several times to be quiet, and to stop banging. But she carried on, getting louder each time. I finally lost it and snapped, "Shut the fuck up!" I'm guessing she wasn't used to people standing up to her, because she said, "What?", and, stupidly, I repeated myself. She instantly flipped the pool table over (it wasn't a full-size one), and then I'd never seen her run so fast. She was up in my face screaming; she pushed me and was threatening to batter me. The staff came straight out of the office and pulled her off me. I was in complete shock and left the room. Once I was in the corridor, I had a panic attack. Fiona, one of the support workers told me to grab my jacket and took me for a walk to get me out of the building.

When I came back, the pool table had been removed, and one of the ovens was smashed. I understand why the pool table was removed, but it seemed unfair to punish everyone for one person's actions.

CHAPTER 23

TENSION

Tensions in the hostel were high after that, and things never really went back to how they had been before. A week or so later, I was on the verge of completing the jigsaw, but two pieces were missing. I didn't think much of it until someone mentioned that they had been deliberately taken, which really annoyed me. While everyone else had been out partying and doing drugs, I'd been doing well to say no to all of that and had managed to keep myself out of trouble, and this is what I got in return. Two of the culprits made a joke out of it, and I told them how childish they were. Perhaps that was stupid, as I ended up in a screaming match that I was never going to win. I can't even remember what else was said, but it resulted in me being chased down the stairs by both of them. Once I was outside, one of them got up in my face, wanting me to hit her. I wasn't that stupid, I'd never hit anyone in my life, but they knew I would get kicked out of the hostel automatically if I did, and that was clearly what they wanted. They got bored of harassing me eventually, and I headed up to Survivors with Amber, who had witnessed the quarrel and was pretty shaken up. After a few days, one of the girls apologized to me, but things were still never the same.

During the second week of September, some of us residents took part in an arts and crafts activity and left our creations to dry in the kitchen, which proved to be a mistake. The next morning, I found mine all ripped up. While I knew instantly who was to blame, I didn't confront them. However, throughout the day I made a few passing comments that whoever had done it was childish, which obviously didn't sit well. One of the staff members confirmed that Georgina had ripped my work up, but told me that I wasn't to say anything because they shouldn't have told me.

That night, when I was at Survivors, I started getting abusive text messages from Georgina. She called me a "pure freak" and a "pigeon face", which still makes me laugh because it doesn't really mean anything. She was also going to "batter me". She tried ringing me a few times and while I didn't answer at first, when I did I put the phone on loudspeaker so Eileen and Christie could hear what she was saying. She proceeded to go on a ten-minute rant about how she wanted to meet me for a fight, and how I should go and kill myself because I deserved to die like Leah did. I thought she was all talk, but Eileen rang the security guard at the hostel and asked them to keep an eye on me.

The next day, Saturday 14 September, I got back from surfing at lunch time and headed straight to the kitchen to make a brew and cook some food with Naythan, another resident. After a few minutes, Georgina and her girl gang came into the kitchen, and started having a go at me. She said that someone had mentioned that I had said whoever ripped the artwork up was childish. She was shouting, and calling me a "stupid dyke" and a "faggot". She was waving a pool cue around, as if she was going to hit someone with it. She wanted me to leave the kitchen and to, "Fuck off and die like Leah did". I can be pretty stubborn, and I didn't think I should be the one to leave.

Fiona, a staff member, came out of the office as soon as she heard the shouting, and asked Georgina for the pool cue. She ended up throwing it at her, and then picked up a pool ball to throw at me. Her friends persuaded her not to throw it, because "I wasn't worth getting kicked out for". She carried on shouting at me saying things like, "Leah deserved to die", and "Go drink yourself to death like Leah did, you deserve it too", and "Go kill yourself". At which point Fiona jumped in, which made the situation worse as they just accused her of favouritism. The security guard had seen things kicking off on the CCTV and was now in the room, too.

Georgina could see I was getting more and more upset with the things she was saying about Leah. I felt like I was on autopilot and swore at her a few times, which she didn't like. She then got up in my face, threatening to hit me. I said something along the lines of, "Just try it." She then said, several more times, that Leah deserved to die followed by, "Go on, hit me, I know you want to." I replied with, "I'm not that stupid," and then she spat in my face and pushed me. Fiona and the security guard hadn't seen her spit because of the angle, but it was all on camera. I was nearly sick, and instantly I was over at the sink, washing my face.

I left the room and went outside for a cigarette, or three. Fiona came down to say, having watched the CCTV back, she knew that Georgina had spat at me.

Georgina came down, and informed me there was now £50 on my head – but I still have no idea what she thought I had done. I went back up to the kitchen to get my tea, and she followed me. She then made a point of making a phone call in front of me, where she told whoever was on the other end that she would pay them £50 to seriously hurt me. That's when I got worried. I knew some of the people she was friends with, and I had no doubt that they wouldn't hesitate in trying to hurt me.

I spoke to both Fiona and the security guard about what had happened. They both said they couldn't tell me what to do, but that I could report what had happened if I wanted to; after all, it was on CCTV and there were plenty of witnesses.

I went to Survivors, and as soon as I told them what had happened, they persuaded me to report it to the police. An officer came to speak to me and I gave him a brief statement; he said they wouldn't be able to do anything until the following day. I knew Georgina was friends with a lot of people, and she also knew I would be at Survivors. The police made sure I got back to the hostel safely, and gave me a direct number in case she tried to start anything again.

That night, I found it even more difficult than usual to sleep. I wasn't overly bothered about being spat at and pushed, as disgusting as it was, but the things she said about Leah were unforgivable and really hurt me. I was angry. Last time she had pushed me, she had later apologized (to avoid punishment). But she'd just done exactly the same again. How did she expect me to react?

I felt bad about reporting Georgina to the police, as I knew she had her own unresolved issues. But her issues weren't an excuse to treat other people the way she did. At some point you have to take responsibility for your behaviour and, more importantly, your life. Especially when the people you are treating so badly have only ever tried to help you.

Georgina was arrested in the early hours of Monday morning, and I was assured she wouldn't be coming back to the hostel. It made me feel much safer, but then my problems got worse.

CHAPTER 24

SNITCH

I was out most of the next day, but I'm a creature of habit, so when I got back, as usual I went to make a brew in the kitchen. I was sitting on the kitchen worktop, watching the TV and drinking my tea, when Georgina's friends all came into the kitchen and started having a go at me. Apparently, "snitches get stitches", and there was now £100 on my head, instead of £50. None of them could understand why I'd reported the assault and threw a barrage of insults at me, saying that I had ruined Georgina's life, and she was threatening to kill herself. I still think now that if any of them had been in my position, they would have done the same thing. It was just a gang mentality: their friend couldn't possibly be in the wrong. Things were getting heated and the staff had come out of the office.

Even though some of them hadn't even been there the previous day, they were adamant that I was in the wrong. I'd provoked Georgina, I'd had my arms up as if I was going to hit her and she felt threatened. I was getting so angry that I couldn't even remember properly. What if I had provoked her? What if she now does something stupid and it's my fault? One of the other staff members assured me that he had watched the footage back and I hadn't provoked her, and I was just to ignore the others. That's not easy though when you have to live with them.

I went back to my room. I was so angry with myself, with them, and with the whole world. I smashed up some of my stuff, and ended up self-harming – I needed the release. I also needed Leah. Leah was way tougher than me, and she would have known what to do. She wouldn't have put up with anyone giving me any trouble.

Over the next few days, whenever I was in the kitchen there were arguments and shouting – the same insults, name calling and blaming on repeat. I was glad I could escape to Survivors, and that I at least had Amber and Naythan on my side.

The next argument came a few weeks later when I was watching *EastEnders*. Two of Georgina's friends came into the kitchen to cook and turned their speaker on really loud. If they had asked if they could have put their music on while they cooked, I would have been fine with it. But they didn't ask, which really annoyed me. How hard was it to ask a simple question?

When my PTSD was at its worst, I really struggled with loud noises, particularly lots of different noises going on at the same time, such as music alongside the TV. It's still something I struggle with if I'm having a bad day, but not to the same extent. This day was already a bad day. I asked, probably in an unpleasant tone, "Can you turn that off? I'm watching TV." And that kickstarted a huge argument.

The stage at which we'd got to with the EMDR therapy meant I was frequently getting super-angry, super-fast, – which I know is no excuse, and I shouldn't have taken it out on other people. They called me names, insulted my appearance and character, and although I shouted and swore back at them, I made sure I didn't get personal. I've never liked people getting personal when they were insulting me, so I knew I couldn't let the anger take over and stoop to that level.

I went back to my room, and was instantly so angry with myself. I couldn't believe I'd let them get to me, and that I'd retaliated. Lisa came to check if I was okay. She knew that I was upset with myself for reacting rather than because of the things they'd said. She asked me if there were any friends I could go see, or speak to. In that moment, the only person I wanted was Leah.

Looking back, I should have walked away from the argument, but it's hard when you're in that environment; and it's hard to explain that environment to someone who's never been there. If you walk away, you're seen as weak, which just makes you even more of a target. The anger caused by the PTSD also didn't help the situation. When you're living in a hostel with so many other young people, who have all been through similar things and are dealing with that in the only ways they know how, it's easy to get consumed by the negativity. You have to try to remember that everyone living there has faced so many problems and been let down by so many different people.

CHAPTER 25

THE WAVE PROJECT

A few months after moving into the hostel, I started volunteering with The Wave Project. Once my own surf therapy had finished, I knew I needed to carry on surfing. The Wave Project meant I could volunteer and help kids get as much out of surfing as I did. I loved seeing their confidence improve and, more generally, how much surfing and the sea helped calm so many of them down. It also meant I got to meet loads of amazing people, who became my best friends. We all had so much in common, and we all loved seeing how surfing improved the kids' lives.

I'd also started working with Go 4 It UK, a local company that helps young people who are out of work get extra qualifications and do work placements to improve their confidence. I'd been persuaded by Fiona to sign up for a first-aid course that Go 4 It were running, which is when I met Jane, who became my key worker. Jane mentioned that Go 4 It could pay for us to do additional qualifications if there was a chance they would improve either our mental health or the chances of us getting a job. I instantly thought of the surf instructor course, and in November, they paid for me to do exactly that.

I was really excited, but also terrified, because I knew my swimming wasn't great and, compared to most people who surfed, neither was my confidence in the water. I was also very aware I hadn't been surfing that long. Joel, who I had met through The Wave Project, was also doing the course with me. We knew on the last day of the course there was a timed indoor swim: we needed to be able to cover 200 metres in five minutes. In the six weeks before the course, Joel and I went swimming every day. When we had started surfing, neither of us could do more than two lengths without stopping, and our fitness was so bad it took us over ten minutes to complete 200 metres. A few days before the course I managed to do 200 metres in 6 minutes and 15 seconds. Joel was faster than me, but still not quite fast enough. There was also a 200-metre sea swim, which Joel and I had been practising; naively we were pretty confident, but we'd only practised on days when the sea was flat. The day before the course started, I found out I was going to be the only girl on the course, which completely freaked me out. I knew Joel would be there, along with Matt, and I told myself that if it got too much I could leave.

The first thing we had to do was a five-minute presentation about ourselves: why we started surfing and why we wanted to do the course. I really surprised myself. Despite being terrified, I stood up and told the others in the room how much surfing had helped my PTSD, and that I wanted to be able to pass that on to other people.

The third day of the course covered surf rescue and beach lifeguarding, which we had to pass to be able to teach surfing. As soon as we got down to the beach, I was panicking. It was one of the choppiest days of the year, with huge waves that we had not thought about when we were practising.

We started off with a warm-up activity: we just had to enter the water, dive under a few waves, and get back out. I went under one wave and the mixture of the freezing water and the tight wetsuit hood round my face panicked me. I got straight out, and Matt followed me. He could tell I was panicking, but he got me to breathe and calmed me down, and then I had another go with him next to me. We did it a few more times and although I was panicking, I managed it. The next part would be the hardest part: the sea swim.

The first instructor paddled 100 metres out to sea on a surfboard, and we all had to swim out, touch the board and swim back. We all set off together, and some of them were straight out there, completely unfazed. As soon as I was in the sea, I panicked. I stopped and went to turn round. Matt caught me and got me to breathe. Once I had calmed down, he persuaded me to have another go, and said he would do it with me. I got under the first few waves to where they weren't breaking as much, still panicking. I couldn't breathe, and I felt so out of my depth. Matt got me to stop where I was, and held my hand while I got my breath. We carried on a bit more, but the waves kept coming and I had to remember to breathe while getting over them. Matt made me feel slightly safer, partly because I knew he was qualified to rescue me, but mainly because of how calming he was – telling me to breathe and not letting go of my hand when I was completely freaking out. We eventually reached the surfboard where one of the instructors was, we had a breather and then turned round. It was even worse now, because we were going back towards the beach and the waves would be breaking on us from behind. Matt never let go of my hand and was constantly reassuring me and telling me to breathe. It took us ages to get back because of a rip, but eventually we got there.

Back on the beach, I literally collapsed. I could have cried, but I was extremely conscious that as the only girl there it wouldn't have looked great. I didn't think I'd be able to do it, and although Matt had held my hand the whole time, I had got through it. This was a big deal. So often the PTSD meant I completely panicked and so didn't even try things. Throughout the week my confidence slowly increased, and I became more comfortable within the group, which they all noticed.

My next challenge came a few days later, on the penultimate day of the course. We were working on rescuing unconscious casualties from the water, which meant us all manhandling each other. I didn't know what was coming, but the instructor asked me to demonstrate as I was the smallest. I was lying next to the board, pretending to be unconscious, when he swam over and got hold of me to pull me onto the surfboard. I froze…

It is happening all over again, he is holding me down and there is nothing I can do.

For the drill, I wasn't supposed to move, so no one noticed, but for a few minutes it was like I was ten years old again. Once that drill was done, I sat out for a while so I could compose myself.

When it came to the timed swim I completely panicked again. It took me over eight minutes, because everything I had practised went out of the window. The breathing, the front crawl, the turns – I lost it all.

Although I failed the swim, I finished the course proud of myself, proud that I had given it my best shot and not given up, and I now had 30 days to work on the swim so I could still pass the course. I went straight back to the hostel to tell Lisa how I'd got on. I was absolutely buzzing that I had got through the week and passed everything but the swim. I could tell that Lisa was buzzing for me too.

CHAPTER 26

INJUSTICE II

On Friday 8 November 2019, the morning after the surf instructor course, I was woken by a phone call from an unknown number. I was absolutely exhausted, and wouldn't usually answer calls from unknown numbers, but I was aware the detectives could call me at any time and I hadn't heard from them in a while. I remember the exact words he used, "Can I come and see you because I've got an update about the case?" I started panicking – that was the line the detective used last time, when they told me they were dropping the case. He told me he would be there as soon as he could, but as soon as I put the phone down I had a feeling I knew what was coming.

I went straight to the office of the hostel. I'm guessing they could tell how panicked I was as I tried to explain what was happening. I sat in the office until the detective got there, and Evie, one of the support workers, made me a brew (tea helps everything, right?). I was so anxious, I had to run back to my room to throw up. Considering he said he would get there as fast as he could, it seemed like forever; I knew it wouldn't have taken him that long to walk directly from the police station.

When he arrived, we sat down in the kitchen-cum-living-room of the hostel, and I couldn't even look at him. I found myself staring at the awful red leather sofa, and feeling the dread completely take over. Just as the detective had done last time around, he started explaining how they couldn't pass every case over to the Crown Prosecution Service if they didn't think there was a chance of them being able to prove it had happened "beyond reasonable doubt".

That phrase is now my most-hated phrase. I couldn't get any words out, but even if I had, I'm not sure what an appropriate response would have been – can you say, "Well, I think that's bloody stupid," to a detective?

I ran to my room for cigarettes and headed straight outside. I punched the wall a few times and then completely lost it; the anger took over. I was sitting on the floor in an absolutely filthy alleyway, too angry to think straight, with members of the public walking past – a definite low point.

The detective spoke to the staff in the hostel, and then came outside to speak to me. He gave me a letter, which basically repeated what he had told me. He said he would get his female colleague to give me a ring in a few days to check how I was doing. I lit another cigarette…

It is happening again – I can't move, I can't scream, I can't do anything.

As I sat there in the filthy alleyway with no regard for the rest of the world, the flashbacks wouldn't stop, I couldn't escape them. It was like my abuser was standing right in front of me, laughing in my face. I punched the wall and went back to my room. I knew what I needed to do to make the flashbacks stop, and I started self-harming. I didn't stop until my arm was completely covered in blood. It was almost like tunnel-vision, I couldn't think about anything else until I'd seriously hurt myself.

There was a knock at my door. I couldn't ignore it, as if it was a member of staff they would worry and enter without permission to do a welfare check. I hadn't had a chance to clean up my arm, so I was in a right state. I opened the door with my arm behind my back, but as soon as I saw Evie, I collapsed onto the floor and she saw what I had done to my arm. She told me that if I cleaned myself up and came to the office, we could go for a long walk.

So, I did. And, although walking was the last thing I wanted to do, it really helped to calm me down and bring me back to the present moment. We walked near the sea, which always helped me.

We were out for a few hours, but as soon as we got back to the hostel the panic rose up again. No matter what I did, the flashbacks wouldn't stop. That evening, we were meant to be having a movie night in the hostel, but I couldn't face it. I knew I needed to go for another walk; the fresh air would help. The conversation with the detective was playing over and over in my head, and all I could think about was "beyond reasonable doubt".

I took only my phone and my cigarettes, and left both my jacket and keys behind. I remember leaving the hostel and walking down the alleyway directly outside it, but the two hours after that are a complete mystery.

The next thing I remember was being back in the alleyway by the hostel, absolutely covered in blood, and unable to say anything. I was terrified. Where had I been? What had I been doing for nearly two hours? Was that my own blood?

I realized I didn't have my keys, and waved at the camera so the security guard could buzz me in, but I didn't even make it through the second door. I don't know if it was all of the blood, or the sheer terror of not knowing where or how I'd spent the past few hours, but I had a sudden, scary, overwhelming feeling, like the whole world was on top of me and crushing me alive. My legs just gave up on me and, before I knew it, I was curled up against the wall without the ability to get any words out. The security guard alerted the staff, and two of them came down and started trying to get me upstairs. I still can't explain it to this day, but I physically couldn't move or speak.

I've since found out that dissociation is a fairly common trauma response, which many people experience to some degree during their lifetime. If our brains can't cope with a particularly overwhelming or stressful feeling or event, dissociation is a way of us being able to disconnect that thought, feelings or event. It's also apparently common for dissociation to result in gaps in your memory, meaning you can't remember chunks of time. It was particularly scary because I'd never experienced anything like it before, and I didn't understand what was happening. Imagine waking up and being covered in blood, not knowing how it got there – it was that level of fear.

Eventually I came round and dragged myself upstairs with the staff, but I was still in a haze. I got cleaned up and I was given an ultimatum: go to Survivors or they would ring the area's mental health crisis team, who previously I'd felt really let down by. They didn't know me and what I'd been through, and previously I'd felt like they didn't really care. I didn't need an ultimatum. They knew I loved Survivors and was comfortable there, and I knew Eileen would be working; but could I really face them all? I couldn't explain the last few hours, where I'd been or what I'd been doing. I knew the crisis team would only make things worse – that was one thing that could be guaranteed.

One of the staff members said she would walk me up to Survivors – perhaps she didn't trust me to get there by myself? As we were walking there, I realized I still had the letter the detective gave me in my pocket, but it was now covered in blood.

I'm not sure what I said to Eileen and Christie, but they knew from the fact that a staff member from the hostel had brought me in that I wasn't okay. I sat in their office, and it didn't take them long to realize I was still bleeding. They asked a few times what had happened, and what was wrong, but I still couldn't speak. I could only cry. They had plenty of tissues, both for the tears and the blood, and all I could manage was to pass them the letter the detective gave me.

When I got back to the hostel at nearly 1am, the security guard told me I'd been put on hourly welfare checks. I completely understood why, but surely they knew that if I didn't sleep at all I would only feel worse? I was told I could sleep, but they would just have to come in and check on me every hour, basically to check I was still breathing. There was no way I would be able to sleep knowing someone – and a man, at that – would be coming into my room while I was asleep. I stayed up all night, and the next day I felt even worse.

The next few weeks are a blur. I wasn't sleeping at night; I was self-harming far more than normal; and I avoided everyone that wasn't either at Survivors or the hostel. I seemed to completely lose the ability to cry, almost as though my emotions had started to shut down. I didn't even surf.

I needed something new, something to get me out of the dark hole that I had once again found myself in.

CHAPTER 27

ACTIVISM

As soon as the last general election was announced in November 2019, I started following it and one of the local candidates closely on Twitter. The candidate followed me back, and I noticed he was also a surfer. We exchanged a few tweets about politics and surfing, and he invited me to a fundraiser at a local pub, where I'd be able to meet other local people who had similar interests, and there would be live music. I hadn't socialized for ages, but I thought it was a good opportunity to be involved with something that mattered. I had started to realize that I didn't want other young people to go through the same things I had been through, and hoped I had the power to try to make a difference once I was in a better place.

I instantly got on really well with Hugo and his partner, Vix, along with so many other people from the local political scene. It was the first time I'd been in a new social situation where I was able to admit that I lived in a hostel; I didn't feel like I had to pretend to be something I wasn't, and I could be myself.

It was nice to be around people that weren't either from the hostel or Survivors, and to have conversations that seemed fairly "normal", whatever that really means. The live music was incredible, and we spoke for hours about politics and surfing. It was also the first time I'd socialized in a pub without feeling like I had to drink, as there was no pressure from anyone.

I and a few others were invited back to the house of a couple called Debbie and Mark for a few games of pool and more drinks. We played "Killer", which I'd never played before, and I definitely overestimated my pool skills. I'd spent hours playing in the hostel with Lisa and Amber, but it was only a tiny table with a plastic cue, so I quickly realized I was absolutely terrible on a full-size table. But we still had a laugh, and I really enjoyed the company.

After that meeting, I knew I wanted to be involved with their election campaign and what they were doing locally. I instantly felt a part of the team, and like we were fighting for the greater good. Knowing I could have an impact locally really pushed me to get outside of my comfort zone.

Over the next few days, I got heavily involved with the campaign. Within a week I was leading teams of canvassers, helping run the campaign office, and even got up at 6am to distribute leaflets at the train station during rush hour. It was crazy how quickly so much changed for me, just within that first week. I had this new-found sense of confidence that I'd never experienced before – the sudden ability to speak to people I didn't know, to knock on random people's doors without knowing who would answer, and to speak to other campaigners on the phone who I hadn't even met yet.

For me, it was not so much about the politics, although we did all believe in the same things, but more about that shared sense of purpose and the feeling of being a part of something much bigger than myself. I really felt connected to these people that I'd only just met because we shared the same principles. They took me under their wing, and I made many amazing friends within just a few short weeks.

One day, on the way back from Whitby where Hugo and I had been for an event, we started chatting about the hostel, mental health and life in general. I had always struggled with men, but I trusted Hugo. Even though I hadn't known him for very long, something about him was just so calming, and I felt like he understood me. Previously, I'd always avoided talking to men if at all possible; and I especially didn't tell men about my past, or the fact that I was living in a hostel, or about the PTSD, let alone the causes of the PTSD. Strangely, I found myself opening up to Hugo, telling him about the previous few years, life in the hostel, and how and why I found myself experiencing homelessness. For me, it was a huge step, putting my trust in a male again. I got emotional, and so did he, and then he gave me a hug. Honestly, I don't think I've ever needed a hug as much as I did that day.

The next few weeks were brilliant. I spent the days campaigning alongside my new friends; I had tea with Debbie, Mark and their family a few times; and a group of us went to the pub. Just having a reason to get out of bed in the morning and the renewed sense of purpose was just what I needed.

During the election campaign, the hostel decided to start weekly life skills sessions, which included things like how to develop healthy relationships and a visit to the local fire station. I was engrossed in campaigning; I had found something I was passionate about and the staff could see how much it had improved my confidence in such a short amount of time. However, I received two written warnings for not attending the sessions. I was furious. I was doing something productive with my time, trying to fight for change in the local area, and I was being told I needed to visit the local fire station. I could understand how it might benefit some of the younger residents, but I really couldn't see how attending would benefit me, especially as I didn't get on with some of the others living in the hostel.

CHAPTER 28

UNCERTAINTY

The manager at the hostel had already promised me I wouldn't have to move on until after Christmas, and, as much of the tension at the hostel had dissipated, I was much more comfortable there. So, it was a massive shock when, during the first week of December, the manager told me that I would be moving the following week, just two weeks before Christmas.

I had no choice as to where or when I was moving.

So much of PTSD is about both control and choice, as when you've experienced any form of abuse you often don't have either. As I have so many traumatic memories in which I didn't have control of situations and my choices were taken away from me, a change in my situation like this was extremely triggering – experiencing emotions or feelings that we associate with trauma can cause us to feel those initial emotions again.

The out-of-control feelings made the nightmares and flashbacks become more frequent and more intense. The block of flats they wanted me to move to was the most notorious of all the blocks the company used, and well known locally for drugs and partying – and earlier that year someone had even been stabbed in the building. The thought of having to live there, but more importantly not feeling safe, filled me with dread.

Over the next two weeks I was given two different moving dates, but the day before each I was told that things had changed so it wouldn't be happening. Eventually, I was told I would definitely be moving on 18 December, exactly one week before Christmas. I'd had my stuff packed up since the first week of December, so I was living out of boxes and bin bags and didn't know whether I was coming or going. There was also some talk of me potentially being able to move into a different, quieter block. Stupidly, I got my hopes up – the different block option never materialized.

I tried to argue my case, explaining that if I didn't feel safe my mental health would deteriorate, but no one was interested. They considered it time for me to move on, and someone else needed my room in the hostel. The manager, along with the staff in the hostel, knew that I would struggle more than usual over the Christmas and New Year period. I'd explained several times that I had specific bad memories on these dates, which would make the PTSD even harder to deal with. If I was still in the hostel there would be staff around, along with planned activities, so I could try to keep myself distracted. But no matter how much I argued, and got other people to argue my case, it didn't change a thing. All of the staff, apart from Lisa, told me I would be fine, and that the block of flats wasn't as bad as everyone said it was. But I was grateful for Lisa's honesty – there is nothing worse than people trying to put a shine on something that you already know is going to be awful.

CHAPTER 29

CHAOS

I had to move all of my things out of my room in the hostel first thing in the morning, but the flat I was moving to wouldn't be available until later in the day, so I dumped my stuff in Amber's room. I knew I had to accept, and then try to deal with what was coming. I went for a cuppa with Lilly and headed back to the hostel, still not knowing how long it would be until I could move my belongings.

As soon as I was told the flat was nearly ready for me to move into, my brother Danny came and picked me and my stuff up and took me to the flat, which was only a few minutes away. As soon as we pulled round the corner into the cul-de-sac, we could hear the music blaring, and the fear gripped me even tighter.

The staff were still there cleaning, but when we arrived there was no electricity and they were cleaning it using the torches on their phones. I had known it was going to be bad, but I didn't anticipate quite *how* bad. The music that was coming from the flat above was louder than I ever could have imagined. Within minutes my anxiety was through the roof; I genuinely didn't know how I was going to cope.

I was assured by the staff that I could ring the security guard at the hostel if there were any problems, and that they had already asked the resident above to turn the music down, but I wasn't reassured. The music wasn't turned down, and played until the early hours of the morning. I stayed at Survivors as late as I could, but I couldn't stay there all night.

The next day I walked down to the hostel to meet Amber for a cigarette. The hostel manager was coming out at the same time as

Amber and asked me how my first night was. I was brutally honest and told her how awful it was. I hadn't felt safe, so why should I pretend I had?

Her response was, "It's not that bad." How would she know? Had she spent the night there? She didn't have a clue about the realities of the situation, and was in no position to tell me what it was really like. She could just finish her shift and go back to the safety of her own home.

During the first few days I had several different people over, but quite honestly it was embarrassing. One of my friends brought me homemade soup a few times to try to cheer me up, but we always ended up escaping to Survivors when the music got too much. A few of my friends from The Wave Project came over one evening, along with my cousins, but again the music was so loud we couldn't even hear each other speak. While it was nice to be able to have visitors (which I hadn't been able to do in the hostel), it was uncomfortable and downright embarrassing when we couldn't communicate because of the noise.

Three days after moving in, Amber and two friends came over for pizza and board games. Shortly after they arrived, we decided to go outside for a cigarette. On opening my door, I realized there was a woman unconscious on the floor, leaning towards the stairs. We didn't know her, but we were concerned that if she moved even slightly, she would fall down the stairs. We rang an ambulance and the security guard from the hostel, and put her in the recovery position. As she started to come around, it was apparent she'd taken an overdose; she didn't even live in the building, and was in fact banned.

The following evening, I was cooking alone in the flat when I suddenly heard shouting and screaming. I instantly ran to make sure my door was locked. I looked out of the window and saw two men approaching the building with their hoods up. As they got closer, they started throwing stones at the window of the flat above mine, and screaming that they would batter whoever was living there. They quickly realized that the main door to the building was unlocked, and before I knew it they were inside and running up the stairs, still shouting. They then tried to break down the door of the man living above me. I rang the security guard at the hostel, who informed me that there was nothing he could do, and if I was concerned, I could ring 101 or 999 if it was an emergency. I heard one of the men shouting that he had a knife, and if the door was put through, he wouldn't hesitate to use it. I rang the police to report it and they said they would send someone as soon as possible; they knew the men were still in the building.

Before long the men left, and as soon as they did, I ran to Survivors. I then got a phone call from the police asking me to let them into the building, forcing me to go back to the flat. I told them what had happened, and they assured me that if the men came back later on I could ring 999 and they would send someone immediately.

The men did come back. Luckily, the downstairs door was locked, but they were still throwing things at the windows. I rang 999 and they said they would send someone. The men carried on throwing things and shouting for nearly 45 minutes, and then gave up. I stayed up until 4am, presuming the police would need me to let them into the building again and that they wouldn't be long, they'd probably just got caught up with something else. Some time after 4am I fell asleep on the sofa, and was woken up at 8:30am with a loud knock on the door from a police officer and member of staff from the hostel. It had taken them 9 hours to respond, which made me feel even more unsafe. What if the door hadn't been locked and the men had got into the building again?

It soon became clear that the man living above me was selling drugs. There were people coming and going at all hours of the day, but they never stuck around for more than a few minutes. He was constantly nipping down to the alleyway just outside the building, past the point that was covered by CCTV, to exchange gear with random people.

Most nights I would ring the hostel to complain about the noise, just to be told they couldn't do anything about noise complaints and I would have to ring the police. The police would then say the same, and that I needed to complain to the local council, but they admitted it could take months for them to act.

I was very grateful for my new-found friendships from the general election campaign, which meant I could escape for a few days over Christmas. I had only been living in the block for five days, but I already needed the break, and Hugo made sure I didn't have to spend Christmas in the flat.

I returned to the flat on 28 December, and then went to meet some of my campaigning friends at the pub for "one drink". Before moving into the flat, I hadn't had a drink since Leah died, because I hadn't been able to bring myself to do the thing that eventually killed her. But once I'd moved into that flat, I started drinking again, and so that "one drink" turned into God knows how many.

When I got back to my flat the neighbours were partying again, and this time there were a lot of people in the building. The situation was starting to really affect my mental health. I wasn't able to sleep at nights, so I was too exhausted to do anything during the days. I sat up most of that night, trying to work out what on earth I could do to change things. Lisa had mentioned helping me search for a private rented flat, but how would I afford the deposit and the first month's rent up front?

Each night the anti-social behaviour got worse, and my tolerance quickly decreased. The lack of sleep was wearing me down, and the constant noise meant I couldn't just sit in my flat and read or do anything that required concentration. Every day for a week, I turned up at the hostel to complain as soon as the staff arrived, and I was usually in a right state.

The parties were getting bigger and more frequent, and they usually lasted until late the following morning. On 10 January, after again turning up at the hostel in despair, a staff member suggested I start to look at private rented flats – social housing in Scarborough was not an option for me as I didn't have a six-month tenancy in my own name.

We rang a few estate agents, who said they'd get back to me. I went to Survivors, still distressed, and two of my friends, Jack and Toby, brought me some food and a brew. Jack commented, "You look knackered mate, what's going on?" I explained the situation in the flat. They could tell how angry I was at the whole situation and the fact that I felt like I couldn't do anything about it. We joked around, and in my cloud of anger and sleep deprivation we came up with a master plan. It meant I would sleep, but it also meant breaking the electric meter of the man living above me. We were only messing about, and I had no intention of actually doing it. We used my key for the electric meter and some paper to craft something the same shape as the meter key, which if inserted into my neighbour's meter would get stuck and he wouldn't be able to top up his electricity. He'd run out eventually, right? It really was only a bit of fun, and making the replica key cheered me up and distracted me for a few hours.

It's strange looking back at that day in January, because I can see my mental health was at an all-time low. I stayed at Survivors until it closed that night, and then headed back to the hell hole that was my flat. When I arrived, all was quiet, which was especially strange for a Friday night. For an hour I managed to sit and read for the first time since I'd moved in. I then got ready for bed and, just as I was shutting my eyes, as if they had timed it... BAM! Music! And within ten minutes there must have been 20 other people in the building.

I left it a while before ringing the security guard at the hostel. Surprise, surprise! He couldn't do anything about a noise complaint, so I had to ring 101. After 20 minutes on hold to 101 they said exactly the same – I had to contact the council for noise complaints. How could they expect anyone to live here? What if I'd had a job and had to be at work early the next morning?

The party showed no signs of calming down, and as usual the noise was making me feel unsafe, triggering flashbacks. I couldn't take it anymore; I was so exhausted and just needed to sleep.

I knew that there was only one thing that would calm me down. So, I self-harmed, badly; worse than I ever had before. The severity wasn't intentional, but with the noise and the flashbacks I got carried away. I needed the noise to stop.

I was at my wits' end. I waited until the bleeding had slowed down slightly, it showed no signs of stopping completely, and I took the replica meter key downstairs. I took note of how much electricity he had left (less than £1, that wouldn't last long), and stuck it in. The music went off instantly, which I hadn't expected, so I ran back upstairs. After bandaging my arm, I tried to sleep. I was so stupid – I could have electrocuted myself or knocked out the electrics for the whole block, but I was so exhausted, I couldn't even think. My intention was only to prevent him being able to top up the electricity again so I could get a few hours' sleep. It turned out that jamming his meter stopped him being able to get any electricity at all.

At 11am the next morning, I woke to banging on my door. He must know it was me who stopped his electricity. I panicked. I really hadn't thought this through. I should have expected this kind of reaction, but what else was I meant to do? I'd asked for help from the hostel and the police, and no one would do anything. I felt I'd had no choice. I'm guessing that before I moved in, no one had complained, so he knew it was me. He was at my door for a good five minutes, threatening to batter me and put my door through. It was stupid of me to expect any different. What did I think he was going to do when he realized I had messed with his meter? In fairness, at 3am and, after not sleeping for days on end, does anyone really have the ability to think things through logically?

I heard him go out, so I went straight to Survivors. I met Toby and Jack, we got some breakfast, and I told them what I'd done. I don't think they could quite believe that I had gone through with it – I couldn't either.

Maybe an hour later, I got a Facebook message from the girl staying in the flat next to mine. Her electricity had gone off too, and the man whose meter I'd broken was also there kicking off. I knew I had to do something because this wasn't fair on her. I asked her to let me know when the man had left the building so I could go back and try to fix the electric supply. I took both Toby and Jack with me, and it soon became apparent that my electricity wasn't working either.

I texted the staff at the hostel to tell them what had happened, and to ask how I should go about fixing it. I had to try to sort out my mess. It looked like he had jammed both mine and the other girl's meters in retaliation, and, although we managed to get the paper out of all of them fairly quickly, including his, none of the electricity came back on. We rang the electric company and tried to reset the meters, just as the man from the flat above me came back with two of his friends. The electric cupboard was right in front of the entrance to the building, so we couldn't avoid them. The three of them started shouting and getting up in our faces – they said they were going to "batter me", "put my windows through" and "petrol bomb my letter box". I didn't know them very well, but I knew some of the people they were friends with and I was genuinely worried they might act on the threats. I was grateful Toby and Jack were with me, but I felt sorry for the girl in the flat next to mine. She didn't deserve all the hassle.

We went back to Survivors and explained to the staff what had happened, and I realized I'd really messed things up. I hadn't felt safe staying there from the beginning, but now I really didn't feel like I could go back. I'd made a bad situation even worse.

I understood that it was completely my fault, but why had the loud music and parties not been dealt with? There was no consideration for anyone else living in the block and for the detrimental effect it was having on my mental health, and so I had snapped. The man had been allowed to live there for nearly two years with no regard for the rules and the impact on the other residents. Since I had moved in, the staff said they were dealing with it, but nothing at all changed and I was just left to suck it up.

The staff in Survivors recommended I go to the police, and as much as I didn't want to (snitches get stitches, remember), I thought at least they might be able to offer me somewhere else to stay, where I would feel safe, which was the only thing I wanted. How wrong was I? The police officer spoke to a member of staff at the hostel, who basically said it was my own fault, so I would have to deal with it.

The police officer recommended I didn't go back to the flat, at which point Toby said I could stay on his sofa. I still wasn't great with men, but I knew Toby pretty well and that he was born female, so I trusted him. I also knew that he was gay, so I knew he wouldn't try to hit on me. I was apprehensive though because he was also staying in temporary accommodation and wasn't allowed guests after 11pm. It meant if I got caught staying there his tenancy would be at risk, and then we'd both be in trouble. He was adamant he wanted to help, and that we could make sure we didn't get caught by staying at Survivors until all the staff from his building had left. I was really unsure, but I knew I wouldn't feel safe back in the flat. I also knew from Facebook that there would be another party in my block later that day.

We went back to my flat and got anything of value, which admittedly wasn't much, along with my duvet and pillows and enough clothes for a few days. We took it all back to Survivors and ordered pizza.

CHAPTER 30

UNDER THE RADAR

The next few weeks were strange. I felt like I was living in a little bubble. I had to pack my things up each day and hide them in case any of Toby's support workers came in; but at the same time we had a right laugh. We spent most mornings drinking tea, smoking and putting the world to rights, then we would go to Survivors for the afternoon. One of us would then cook something or we'd order food and head back to Survivors. I'd been given a holographic Rubik's Cube jigsaw for Christmas, which we stayed up most nights doing. Even though I was sleeping on a sofa, it was fantastic being able to catch up on sleep, and I actually felt safe.

Later that week, on the Wednesday, I noticed that my arm had gone a funny colour and could potentially be infected. It wasn't healing as it should, and I was aware that it was far worse than usual.

I knew Eileen had previously worked as a nurse, so I asked her to check it, and she was worried too. It was embarrassing having to admit what I'd done, but I knew Eileen wouldn't judge me, and would understand why I'd felt like I didn't have any other choice. She wanted me to get it checked out, but I was terrified of being judged. I didn't want to have to explain everything to someone I probably hadn't met before – although over the years I'd met most local medical professionals from outings with Leah and from X-rays after punching walls. Eileen reassured me, but I wasn't convinced. She'd phoned the local GP and told them I would be coming in. I didn't want to go, but I knew if I didn't, after Eileen had gone out of her way to help me, she'd be disappointed – and I didn't like disappointing Eileen. Once I was there, it was fine. An hour and lots of steri-strips later, I headed back to Survivors.

I spent nearly four weeks on Toby's sofa. To this day, I'm not sure if his support workers knew I was there and just decided not to say anything. As chaotic as it was having to leave early and hide all of my belongings, for the majority of the time I enjoyed staying with him, although I think at times we really got on each other's nerves. Being there meant that on bad days I didn't turn back to drink, drugs or self-harm.

I knew I had to get through my birthday on 21 January, which was going to be a big challenge. The previous year I hadn't been sober, so I had managed to block the bad memories out.

Everyone at Survivors remembered it was my birthday and made the day really nice for me. The day was chilled out until the early evening when we were back at Toby's. I had planned to go out for tea, but just as I was getting out of the shower it happened again...

It is one of my birthdays. I tell him to stop it, he won't listen. It hurts. I don't understand what is going on.

It really messed with my head, because I'd got through most of the day without any hiccups. This really set me back, and it took me ages to calm down. Once I had, we ordered Chinese takeaway and then went for a walk near the sea. Later on, we went to Survivors, where we had cake and drank copious amounts of tea. At the end of the day, I was proud that I'd just about got through it without turning to harmful coping mechanisms.

While I was staying at Toby's I came across an event on Twitter – it was looking for local people to share their stories at a "Human Library" event, with influential people from across the town, including town councillors. I knew from the general election campaign that I wanted to help other people in similar situations to myself, and I realized this was my chance. I had to let the people with the power to make a difference know what the system is really like for young people who find themselves experiencing homelessness. I sent an email.

I still went for coffee with Debbie most weeks, which was lovely, and regularly saw other people from the election campaign. It was nice being able to socialize again, and not feeling like I had to hide from the world.

Just after my birthday, I found out I had been awarded the Personal Independence Payment (PIP) benefit, because of the PTSD. This meant I could now afford to get a private rented flat. I was over the moon. One of the staff members from the hostel arranged for me to see one, and they came with me to view it, but I felt like they were trying to push me into it, and I didn't really know the sorts of things I should be looking for. I was aware that they wanted me to move on – their lives would certainly be easier once I had and they didn't have to deal with me anymore. But I didn't want to jump at the first place I liked and then find something majorly wrong with it; I wasn't going to let them push me into anything. I did really like the first one; it was small, which was perfect for me; it wasn't far from town, but was in a quiet area and there was unlikely to be any trouble. I arranged to see a few more myself with one of my friends, but none of the others were suitable. There weren't many options that were within my budget, and where the landlords would accept tenants on housing benefit and Universal Credit – and all of them required a guarantor, which I didn't have yet. I knew I wanted to look at the first one again, so I went back with Hugo to get his opinion. I still loved it, and so did Hugo. We went to get some food and talked it through, and I decided I was going to apply for it.

CHAPTER 31

NEW BEGINNINGS

As I had to apply for the flat, there was still a chance the landlord could turn me down. Luckily, he didn't, and I was able to move in on 3 February 2020. Mark picked me and my stuff up from Toby's flat, and we went to collect the keys from the estate agent. It was the most surreal experience, knowing that I was finally going to have my own place with a proper tenancy agreement. I couldn't be asked to leave with hardly any notice. I don't think I've ever climbed five flights of stairs as fast. Mark helped me carry all of my boxes and bags up the stairs, and I started unpacking.

If you've never experienced the fear and uncertainty that comes with not knowing where you will be sleeping from one week to the next, it's hard to understand the feeling of relief that comes with knowing you now have your own flat. I could finally relax. I didn't have to pack my stuff up each morning to hide it, or share a kitchen with loads of other people. I didn't have to listen to arguments and fights, or to people who were either drunk or high. I didn't have to listen to the emergency services arriving at every hour of the day and night. It was an inexplicably good feeling.

That first night, I slept the best I had in years. But when I woke up, I got out of bed and instinctively started packing my things. It wasn't until I saw my keys on the floor that I realized I no longer had to.

CHAPTER 32

THE POWER OF SOCIAL MEDIA

Then things started to get really strange. For years, I had been an avid Twitter user, and I tweeted about loads of things: surfing, football, social injustice, and politics during the general election.

The day I moved into my flat, I posted the following on Twitter.

'After been (sic) classed as homeless for 403 days

Today I've moved into my very own flat ☝️' - @h_green21
13:54- 03 Feb 20

Within a few hours, it had over 3,000 likes and 150 retweets, and for a week that number kept on growing. People from all over the world were commenting, wanting to send me things for the flat, and wanting to hear more about my story.

That same week, someone who had seen that tweet tagged me in a post on Twitter; the original post was from an editor for *Metro* newspaper who was looking for real-life stories of people who had overcome adversity. I saved the email address, but didn't think I'd end up doing anything with it.

A few days later, I found myself sitting in Survivors, opening a Google doc on my laptop, and typing. I didn't really know what I was writing about, but it felt like a good thing to do. I ended up writing over 2,000 words. I emailed the editor at *Metro*, with a brief overview of my situation, not really expecting to hear back. I presumed they must have got thousands of people wanting to write about how they have overcome various forms of adversity, and they couldn't publish everything. I had an email back the next day, saying they'd like to publish it and how soon could I have a draft done. I'd already completed a draft, but theirs needed to be a maximum of 700 words, which is where the hard work started.

The piece was published on 15 February 2020, 12 days after I had moved in. Once I knew it was going to be published, my anxiety went through the roof. I'd written it without any real intentions, but here I was, about to share my deepest, darkest secrets with the world. Letting everyone I knew and, frankly, anyone with access to the internet, that I had been sexually abused, and then assaulted – never mind the drinking, the drugs and the self-harm. I started getting second thoughts – did I really want the whole world to know?

After Leah died, a group of students had painted a mural upstairs in Survivors in memory of her. There were butterflies, rainbows, lots of purple (her favourite colour), and some of her favourite quotes. I went and sat upstairs with the mural so I could feel close to her. It hit me that she was the main person I wanted to show around my flat, but I couldn't. At that moment, I knew how proud she would have been, but it was so hard not having her there to celebrate with me. Leah and I had always spoken about what we would do once we had "dealt with our stuff", as she called it – once we were both in a better place and had permanent accommodation. We both knew we wanted to do something that would help other people, we just hadn't figured out exactly what that would entail. I knew she would have encouraged me to publish the article, so I had to go ahead with it, even if it was just for her. Knowing that if just one person read the article and felt slightly less alone, I would be happy.

I was a nervous wreck on publication day; but seeing it go live, with my name on the byline, was the best feeling in the world. Over the next few days I received hundreds of comments, messages, emails, and even got a retweet from author Matt Haig (my idol), which was so reassuring. It was such a good feeling to have people messaging me to say thank you for sharing, and that they'd been through, or knew people who had been through, similar things.

Two days later, an editor from the *Independent* got in contact, asking if I would write something similar for them, but focused more on how I thought we could solve homelessness. This piece had a deadline: I had two days to write it, but I was up for the challenge.

I was in bed on the morning of 20 February, scrolling through Twitter (bad habit I know!), when I got a new notification.

Congratulations to you @h_green21!!! You have been nominated for the Positive Role Model Award for Gender at The National Diversity Awards 2020 in association with @ITVnews! You can vote for Hannah by visiting nationaldiversityawards.co.uk/nominate #NDA20 #Vote

I genuinely turned my phone off, and then back on again. It was still there. I got showered and dressed and went straight to Survivors. I showed Eileen and she was buzzing, but I was still struggling to believe it. I really didn't understand why I had been nominated – only one article had been published so far.

Later that day, the article in the *Independent* was published. I tweeted a link to it and got a reply from the founder of Invisible People, a US-based charity who were looking for a UK-based writer to write about homelessness. It was another perfect opportunity that I wasn't going to say no to; it felt like the stars were aligning.

Within three days of the award nomination, I'd written for *DOPE Magazine*, been featured in the *Yorkshire Post* and *Scarborough News*, and received interview requests from two radio stations. The most surreal part was the photoshoot for the *Yorkshire Post*, which we did on the beach in Scarborough with a surfboard – that was definitely a moment I'll never forget.

CHAPTER 33

"IF WE DON'T TELL OUR STORIES, WHO WILL?"

The Human Library event that I'd enquired about was on 24 February, less than a month after I'd moved into my flat. I'd written about my story a few times by this point, but I hadn't *spoken* about it, which felt like a completely different ball game. What drew me to this event was the opportunity to speak to the town's key decision makers, including the head of Scarborough Borough Council. I felt like my experiences mattered, and I wanted to try to change things for other young people going through similar things.

I'd never been much good at talking about anything, so I turned up and was ridiculously nervous. I had a brew, then started to panic and nearly legged it. I went outside where it was quieter, and Jude, a woman who I had met at a prep event the week before, was out there. I already felt connected to Jude because she told me she was a Nightstop host in London; she could tell how nervous I was. She said I didn't have to take part if I didn't want to, then gave me a pep talk: "You've got a story that needs telling, you can do this." This persuaded me that my story did, in fact, need telling, and I was the only one who could do that. Now, when I reflect on the past few months, it's obvious that if Jude had not given me that pep talk, I wouldn't be where I am today – and I'm extremely grateful for that.

As soon as we started, the anxiety disappeared, and it was the best feeling ever, knowing I was speaking to decision makers within the town council and from local charities, and that what I was saying could influence the work they did in the future.

After the event I spoke to Jude, and it turned out her company, sounddelivery, was holding a conference – Social Media Exchange 2020 – in a few weeks' time in Newcastle. I'm not sure exactly how it came about, but I left the Human Library event with an invitation to attend, which was very exciting.

Just before moving into my flat, I'd finished the EMDR therapy with Karen and been discharged from their services. It was apparent that, although the EMDR therapy seemed to have helped a bit, there were still a lot of things I had to work through. I decided I would start to see a counsellor at Scarborough Survivors. The first session, which was just an assessment, was the same day as the Human Library event. And – Oh my God! – even the assessment was tough.

I knew there were a lot of things that I'd still never spoken about but needed to, or else they'd haunt me in years to come, yet it was such a tough step. I always find the first therapy session the hardest, because I have to try to open up to someone new.

I've always struggled to show emotion, especially in front of people I don't know well, and I spent the first two counselling sessions feeling like I needed to cry but being completely unable to. After the second session, it was also becoming clear that the coronavirus was starting to sweep Europe, and there was talk of lockdowns like those introduced in Italy. A lockdown terrified me – I'd made so much progress in only a few months, and I thought that if I was unable to go to Survivors and see my friends, all that progress would go down the drain.

CHAPTER 34

STAND UP

I went up to Newcastle on the train on 4 March for Social Media Exchange 2020, the same day my article with Invisible People — "What Being Homeless Has Taught Me About My Mental Health" — was published. That day, sitting on the train on my own, was the first time I'd thought, "I'm actually proud of myself." I stayed overnight at Hugo and Vix's home, and headed to the conference the following morning. I was so far out of my comfort zone the whole day, but it was still incredible. I got to meet so many amazing people from all over the country, some of whom I have kept in contact with.

Most of the day I was too nervous to ask any questions, but one session involved a very powerful talk from a woman who had also experienced homelessness, along with various other forms of social injustice. She spoke to us about her experiences of working the streets in Hull and of being in prison. I found her really inspiring and, because it was a small session, I managed to pluck up the courage to ask her advice on telling a personal story to an audience.

I had been asked to speak at an event on International Women's day on 8 March, but thankfully it wasn't going to be a huge event. It was to raise money for Independent Domestic Abuse Services, the charity that my ISVA (independent sexual violence advisor) had worked for, so it was a cause close to my heart. But the fact that I knew most of the people attending made it slightly scarier. On the day, I stood up to speak and was nearly sick. I was shaking, and worried I wouldn't be able to get the words out. But then, it just seemed to happen. The time flew by, and even the most difficult parts flowed. It was extremely empowering to stand up and tell my story in front of that many people, and it left quite a few people in tears.

On 11 March, I spoke again at a political rally which had a slightly bigger audience. Speaking in front of a sitting MP was especially memorable, and when he congratulated me on a "great speech" and Hugo said he was proud of me, I was on the verge of tears. I'm not sure what it is about that phrase, but when people tell me they are "proud of me", it makes me feel extremely emotional.

CHAPTER 35

LOCKDOWN

The political rally was the last "normal" event I attended before lockdown was announced. The coronavirus had started to spread fairly quickly across the UK, and it was declared a pandemic by the World Health Organization the following day, so we knew it was only going to get worse.

I had started to panic. I knew what was coming – potentially months of isolation and not being able to socialize. The PTSD means I always imagine the worst-case scenario, so I'd already fully stocked my freezer before the rest of the country started to panic buy, just in case. My biggest fear was Survivors having to shut, because I genuinely thought I wouldn't cope without it and that my recovery would go completely down the drain. I was sure that I'd end up drinking and taking drugs again – what else was I meant to do without Survivors?

Part of my fear was around getting ill. So much of PTSD is about being in control, and previous experiences of being ill have made me feel very out of control, making the PTSD worse. Although getting seriously ill with the coronavirus was unlikely because of my age and health, it wasn't unheard of.

I was also concerned about my sister, Meg. She had been working on a cruise ship for nearly six months, and it was becoming clear that cruise ships were quickly becoming epicentres of the coronavirus. She has bad asthma, and although her ship hadn't appeared on the news as one of the ones that was stranded and unable to dock, I was still panicking.

I was also anxious that my counselling would have to stop, as I'd only just started it. I didn't want to be completely alone, with all this unresolved stuff still buzzing around my head. How on earth would I deal with it all?

It felt like each night we were having the same discussions in Survivors about the number of coronavirus deaths and potential lockdowns, and everyone was equally anxious. I had started volunteering in Survivors in January, and on 15 March I started volunteering in the Crisis Cafe as well. I absolutely loved it, particularly as the Crisis Cafe had done so much to help me over the previous year.

On 16 March I got a phone call from Meg. All the cruise ships had been ordered back to docks, and she and her boyfriend were being flown home in a few days, which was such a relief.

After an anxiety-filled week, on Sunday 22 March the decision was taken to close Survivors until further notice. It was a really emotional night, and not knowing when I would see Eileen and Christie again was really, really tough; I had seen them most days for the past year. I wasn't prepared for not having my counselling session on the Monday either, as I had convinced myself that I would probably have one more before they decided to shut Survivors. I had only just started, and I was actually starting to open up, and then it was over just like that. I had decided that, once Survivors shut, I would go into my own "lockdown", even if the rest of the country didn't, just to minimize my own paranoia around getting ill.

The first few days I really struggled; I was panicking and hated the uncertainty of not knowing how long the restrictions would continue for. The anxiety meant I was struggling to eat and sleep, and the nightmares were so much worse than usual. I really didn't know how I was going to get through.

Then something strange happened. During that first week of lockdown, the government announced the "Everyone In" scheme to provide emergency accommodation for rough sleepers for the duration of the pandemic. Three days later, a local journalist read one of my posts online and I was invited to take part in my first TV interview on That's TV North Yorkshire. I spoke about my own experiences of homelessness and about the government's decision to house all rough sleepers. Seeing myself on television was another completely surreal moment.

I started lockdown with the ambition of creating daily fitness videos that people could do from home; however, a combination of my awful internet connection and slowly depleting motivation meant this only lasted a few days. I decided to stop putting pressure on myself, because no one really knew how to deal with what we were experiencing.

I struggled through the second week of lockdown. The uncertainty was the worst part – watching what was happening in other countries and seeing what was to come, and not knowing when I could see my friends again. I got daily (sometimes several a day) phone calls from Eileen or Christie, which kept me on a relatively even keel; but I couldn't help thinking that the longer lockdown went on, the more my mental health would deteriorate.

On week three of lockdown, I received an email from an editor at Novara Media, asking if I'd write something for them, as I'd been recommended by another editor. It was a really proud moment, knowing that someone thought enough of my writing to put my name forward to other editors. The piece turned into my first feature; I spoke to people who had been housed in hotels thanks to the Everyone In scheme, along with charities working on the front line.

The same day, my second Invisible People piece was published, on the topic of affordable housing and homelessness prevention. It was great to get the opportunity to go from just writing about my own story to writing about other people's.

That was when lockdown changed for me. Partly because I realized that no one knew how long lockdown would last, and that I could either slowly watch my mental health deteriorate or make the most of the time and try to be productive. Secondly because I think the adrenaline of all these cool opportunities took over and I was suddenly on autopilot. I forced myself to get up early every day and to treat it like a proper working day. I wrote every day, and I grafted harder than I ever had. A lot of the articles I wrote were never even pitched to editors; but I learnt a lot about the processes involved in journalism, and found myself applying for journalism scholarships and training programmes.

I was almost able to turn my emotions off – there was nothing I could do about them anyway, right? Homelessness taught me I had to adapt and get on with things even when I knew I couldn't change them, so that's what I did.

When things were bad growing up, I would lose myself in books for hours and hours, it was an escape. I always knew that, one day, I would write my own book. Before lockdown, in Survivors I had joked about writing a book if lockdown happened. I never imagined what type of book it would be, or that it would actually even happen, but now I found myself writing it.

Things then took another strange turn. I received a Twitter message from a journalist at BBC *Breakfast* asking if I would do an interview. I appeared on the show two days later, and spoke about my experiences of going from experiencing homelessness and living with other people, to being "locked down" and completely on my own. The following week I was asked for another interview, again by BBC *Breakfast* but this time on coping with lockdown as a young person with PTSD. The responses to my appearances were fantastic, and knowing that by speaking out about my own experiences I was helping other people was really empowering.

The following few weeks were a rollercoaster. I wrote guest blog posts and was given more paid writing opportunities. I also took part in podcasts and "Instagram lives", and was asked to speak at my first webinar. The webinar was for the Centre for Homelessness Impact, a charity that champions the use of evidence and data to achieve a world without homelessness. Before lockdown, I had spoken to them about the possibility of me speaking at one of their summer events, but all events were now cancelled due to the pandemic. Instead, I was invited to speak at a webinar as part of their "Covid-19 Talk Series", alongside Dr Emma Williamson, on the topic of limiting trauma during the pandemic.

Part of me felt guilty – while so many people were struggling, losing jobs and loved ones because of the virus, I was finally finding my feet. I had spent so much of my life in chaos, fear and uncertainty that it felt like such a welcome break – a period of calm where I could catch up with the rest of the world.

The webinar was amazing. Being given the opportunity to speak in front of so many influential people and frontline workers, who could actually take what I was saying and change the way their organizations worked, was a privilege.

I agreed to write a follow-up blog post that would summarize the things we had spoken about in the webinar, along with answering any questions that the attendees had. That blog post is still the piece of writing I am most proud of.

Just after the blog was published, I was on the Centre for Homelessness Impact's website, just generally having a look at the work they were doing. I really liked the ethos and culture of the organization, and they seemed to be doing really influential work within the sector. I found myself on the jobs page of their website, but it was empty.

Three days later, I received an email saying that the centre would like to work with me on an ongoing basis. WHAATTTT????!!!! Obviously, I jumped at the chance. Having the opportunity to really make a difference, influence professionals and use my experiences to create change was absolutely incredible. Again, I felt a pang of guilt – many people were losing jobs during lockdown, yet I was being offered one!

A few weeks later I took part in another webinar, this time for North Yorkshire Sport on the importance of physical activity for our mental health, but specifically on how surfing had helped me. A few more of my articles were published, including a feature about the effect of lockdown on individuals who were drug dependent. I was also interviewed on Radio York.

A few weeks into lockdown and the UK experienced its first heat wave of 2020. Pre-lockdown, I didn't wear short sleeves in public, and even very rarely in private, because I was so ashamed of my self-harm scars. It annoyed me that I cared so much about people I didn't even know judging me. Why do people judge how others deal with things they've never experienced?

My flat was high up in the block, which meant it was ridiculously hot, so I found myself wearing short sleeves at home pretty much all the time. As lockdown progressed and the temperature carried on climbing, I wore long sleeves less and less – I was on my own, why did it matter?

One day, towards the end of May, I finished writing another feature for Novara Media and headed out for a walk on the beach. It wasn't until I got to the beach that I realized I'd left my hoodie at home, and I hadn't even thought about covering my arms. I panicked at first and was about to head home, until I realized that, because we were still in lockdown, there was hardly anyone about – the beach that was usually packed at that time of year was now empty.

Over the next few weeks, while Scarborough was empty of the usual tourists, I ventured out in short sleeves more often, and slowly became comfortable with it until I reached the point where I didn't feel the need to wear long sleeves at all. Wearing short sleeves again also stopped me from self-harming when I was having a bad day, which I knew would then start the shame-cycle all over again.

CHAPTER 36

BIGGER THINGS

I started my job with the Centre for Homelessness Impact on Tuesday 16 June 2020 on a two-day-a-week contract.

A few weeks after starting my new job, another journalist got in contact. She wanted to speak to me about my positive experiences during lockdown: starting a new job and my writing journey. They wanted to put me on TV, which I agreed to, and only then did I find out I would be speaking to Victoria Derbyshire. It was complete madness! I'd watched Victoria Derbyshire conduct an interview with some of the men who exposed the sexual offender Barry Bennell, and had admired her ever since. I appeared alongside another lady who was a publicist, and in a strange turn of events she got in contact after the show saying she'd like to be *my* publicist for my writing and eventually my own book! It felt – and still does feel – like I'm living in a dream!

I absolutely love my new job; it is everything I hoped it would be, and more. The opportunity to collaborate with academics, professionals and frontline workers to try to create real change is unbelievable.

Soon after starting my job, the organization held an "Impact Festival" over five weeks. I worked full time during the festival and, although I've always struggled with sleep, for the first time in years I slept properly, at reasonable times and for more than a few hours at once. It was probably due to exhaustion, and unfortunately it didn't last, but it was a temporary bonus, nonetheless.

I was grateful when the lockdown restrictions eased slightly, and I could meet people outside, as long as we socially distanced. It was great being able to see friends and family again after only having virtual contact for so long. I also found that I really did no longer care what people thought of my scars, and without even thinking about it went out regularly in short sleeves.

CHAPTER 37

ANNIVERSARIES

I quickly settled into my job and I was loving it, but another challenge was approaching. Since lockdown had eased slightly and I was able to see my friends again, I found that slowly I was starting to feel again. I was starting to notice feelings that I had managed to switch off for several months. It was strange, and I didn't quite know how to deal with them. A trauma anniversary and the one-year anniversary of Leah's death were going to fall within four days of each other, and I had no idea how I was going to get through them. Survivors was still shut, so we couldn't do anything in Leah's memory.

I had spent so many years telling myself that the abuse never happened, or that it wasn't that bad, or that it was my fault, that the previous year, as a result of therapy, was the first time that I was particularly conscious of this trauma date. It had been a tough day, but I don't remember much of it because I resorted to drugs and alcohol to get me through. So, this year was the first year that I was both aware of the date and sober.

I hadn't slept well for a few days, partly due to the fear of nightmares and partly due to the anxiety of expecting the upcoming Saturday to be the hardest day. However, on the Friday I woke up in a complete panic. I couldn't breathe...

I am 11 years old. It is his birthday and we are at a swimming pool in York. That doesn't stop him. Nothing stops him.

After a few hours and lots of caffeine, I sat in front of my computer and questioned how on earth I was going to get through the rest of the day. I was part of a team running an online festival, which meant Zoom calls with professionals from all over the world.

Fairly early on, I got a message from my colleague and friend, Faye, asking me if I was doing okay and if I could update something on the website. For the first time, I didn't even think about my reply and was brutally honest. I told her I was having a tough time and wasn't quite sure how to deal with it.

I'm so glad I was honest, because it meant we had a good chat and I was able to face the next few days with a completely different mindset. The main thing that stuck with me from that conversation, were Faye's wise words: she said that we can never stop negative thoughts from coming, and sometimes we just have to ride them out; if we try to stop them, we just give them more power. It's as if someone tells you to not think about a pink elephant – the first thing you will picture is a pink elephant. By letting our thoughts *be*, they pass much faster than by giving them our time. She also reminded me that, no matter how successful we are, or how confident we appear to outsiders, negative thoughts are something that everyone has to battle with.

Her advice also made me reflect on PTSD. I can't stop the flashbacks and the nightmares, and, looking back, if professionals ever asked, "Did you have nightmares last night?", I would instantly start thinking about them and give them more of my headspace. I have to learn to accept that some dates are always going to be worse than others, but that's okay.

Lockdown also meant that for the first time in what seemed like forever, I was able to seriously think about the future and what I wanted from life. I spent years thinking I wouldn't make it to my 21st birthday, let alone my 23rd or 24th, so suddenly being able to see a future which wasn't bleak and looked hopeful was on another level. I could see I still had a lot to work through, but that with time some of the stuff I'd been carrying around for years would no doubt get lighter.

I wasn't sure the EMDR had worked. Whilst I knew that I was now far more able to deal with my memories of "that night", and the flashbacks and nightmares of that event were less intense, they still happened. Unfortunately, the memories from my childhood are still just as intense and the flashbacks and nightmares show no signs of improving. Having said that, I am in a much better place and have so many positive things going on that it's much easier to deal with them when they happen, and to not be consumed by them for as long.

CHAPTER 38

WHO KNOWS WHAT'S NEXT?

It's safe to say that writing this book kept me busy and distracted for the majority of the first lockdown. When I didn't have access to counselling, although I was on autopilot, I think writing was a way of me getting my thoughts and feelings out of my head. But, at the time of writing this chapter, we have reached the point of lockdown where a few of my emotions are starting to boil over, and I cannot wait for the counselling to start again. Unfortunately, I don't know when that is likely to happen. For the first time in my life, I feel like I'm in a good place and ready to face up to the challenges that counselling poses.

I've done a lot of speaking engagements over the past few months, and a question I have been asked on several occasions is, "Has the PTSD gone?" Many people presume that, as if by magic, I could be "cured". PTSD can be a lifelong condition, and I may experience it for the rest of my life. But my experiences this year have taught me that my PTSD in no way defines me, just like having experienced homelessness does not define me. However, I do think it is important, for me at least, to use these experiences to try to create change. I am still by no means "okay", and I will never forget the things that have happened to me; but I am working on them, and I am slowly moving towards a place where I can live with them.

Be the change you wish to see in the world
– Mahatma Gandhi

ACKNOWLEDGEMENTS

Writing this book has been one of the hardest things I have ever done. I have a long list of people to thank as, without their incredible support, it would not have been possible.

First and foremost: Eileen Quigley, Christie Beautyman, Andrea Woolcott, Sarah Peirson and everyone else at Scarborough Survivors. Without you guys I wouldn't still be here to write this book. Likewise, Ruth Matthewson – although my PE degree now seems slightly irrelevant, meeting you kept me alive.

I am forever indebted to my therapist, Karen Beale, for never giving up on me when I'd given up on myself. You made me see that I was more than the things I had been through.

Hugo Fearnley, you believed in me when I felt like the world had given up on me. Without your help in getting my flat, I definitely would not have been able to achieve everything I have this year, so thank you.

I have to give a shout-out to Lisa Till, for helping me get through my time in the hostel. The endless games of pool and multiple brews helped me stay sober, which made all the difference.

Jude Habib, thank you for making me believe that my story mattered, and that I could make a difference.

I am immensely grateful to Neville Southall for following and supporting me on my journey over the past few years; your support means the world and I couldn't have done it without you.

A special thanks also goes to Debbie and Mark Gordon, for everything they have done for me, from helping me move into my flat to the days spent playing with Premier League Football cards – you guys are the best.

My surfing pals – Matt, Karen, Terri, Caitlin, Shelby, Charli, Sarah, Sam, Lucy, Paul, Siobhan, Vanessa and, of course, everyone at Dexter's Surf Shop – I am truly blessed to have you all in my life.

Lilly Allenby, thank you for always telling it like it is. Everyone needs someone like you.

Thank you to every single one of my colleagues at the Centre for Homelessness Impact. It is a privilege to work with you all. A special thanks has to go to Faye Greaves for the constant words of wisdom, and to Lígia Teixeira, for putting so much faith in me.

A special thank you also goes to Sarah Dangar – your messages and support helped me get through lockdown.

I am grateful for all of my summer camp friends, but especially Mailén, Zoé, Hannah, Marta, Wally and José.

All of my politics friends – there are far too many of you to mention but you know who you are.

A huge thank you also has to go to everyone at the Blagrave Trust; Jules, Dan and the team at Five in a Boat, and Rich Maw at Infocus Photographic.

Last, but my no means least, I would like to thank my family; I love you guys.

A theme throughout this book has been tea, so I also need to give a massive shout-out to Yorkshire Tea – you got me through the late nights, early mornings and the stress of writing this page.

ABOUT CHERISH EDITIONS

Cherish Editions is a bespoke self-publishing service for authors of mental health, wellbeing and inspirational books.

As a division of Trigger Publishing, the UK's leading independent mental health and wellbeing publisher, we are experienced in creating and selling positive, responsible, important and inspirational books, which work to de-stigmatize the issues around mental health and improve the mental health and wellbeing of those who read our titles.

Founded by Adam Shaw, a mental health advocate, author and philanthropist, and leading psychologist Lauren Callaghan, Cherish Editions aims to publish books that provide advice, support and inspiration. We nurture our authors so that their stories can unfurl on the page, helping them to share their uplifting and moving stories.

Cherish Editions is unique in that a percentage of the profits from the sale of our books goes directly to leading mental health charity Shaw Mind, to deliver its vision to provide support for those experiencing mental ill health.

Find out more about Cherish Editions by visiting cherisheditions.com or by joining us on:
Twitter @cherisheditions
Facebook @cherisheditions
Instagram @cherisheditions

Cherish
EDITIONS

ABOUT SHAW MIND

A proportion of profits from the sale of all Trigger books go to their sister charity, Shawmind, also founded by Adam Shaw and Lauren Callaghan. The charity aims to ensure that everyone has access to mental health resources whenever they need them.

You can find out more about the work Shaw Mind do by visiting their website: shawmind.org or joining them on

Twitter @Shaw_Mind
Facebook @ShawmindUK
Instagram @Shaw_Mind